Gdańsk

Lech Krzyżanowski

Gdańsk

**From the Hanseatic League
to Solidarity**

© RV Reise- und Verkehrsverlag GmbH
Berlin · Gütersloh · Leipzig · München · Potsdam · Stuttgart

Photo on front cover: The Crane Gate, Mauritius/Weber
Cartography: RV Reise- und Verkehrsverlag GmbH, Berlin
Gütersloh · Leipzig · München · Potsdam · Stuttgart
Illustrations: Volkmar Janicke, München: p. 2, 23, 43, 47, 69;
Wacław Górski, Toruń: page 6/7, 10, 12, 13, 14/15, 16, 17, 18/19,
20, 21, 24, 25, 26, 27, 28, 29, 31, 34/35, 37, 44, 45, 49, 50, 51,
53, 54, 57, 59, 61, 62, 64/65, 68, 71, 73, 74, 75, 77, 78/79, 81, 82,
83, 85, 86, 89, 90/91, 92, 93, 95; Elżbieta Kuźmiuk, Warszawa:
page 33, 39.
Author: Dr. Lech Krzyżanowski, Warsaw
English Translation: Eliza Lewandowska, Warsaw
Idea and series conception: Prisma Verlag GmbH, Munich
Editing, coordination: Prisma Verlag GmbH, Munich, with the
assistance of GeoCenter Warsaw
Cover layout: Prisma Verlag GmbH, Munich

Typesetting: Buchmacher Bär, Freising
Reproduction: Repro Ludwig, Zell am See
Printing: Łódzkie Zakłady Graficzne

ISBN 83-86146-38-9

Contents

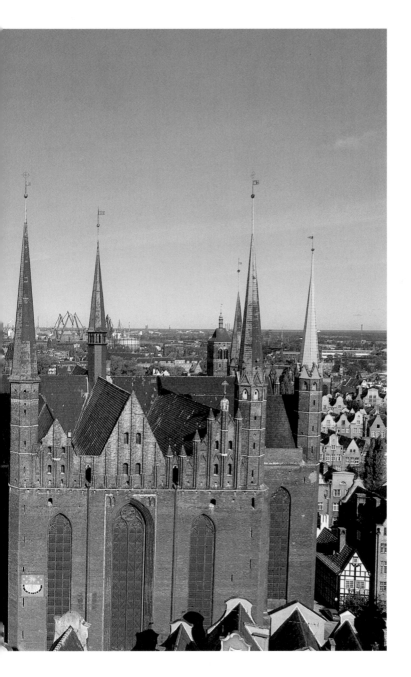

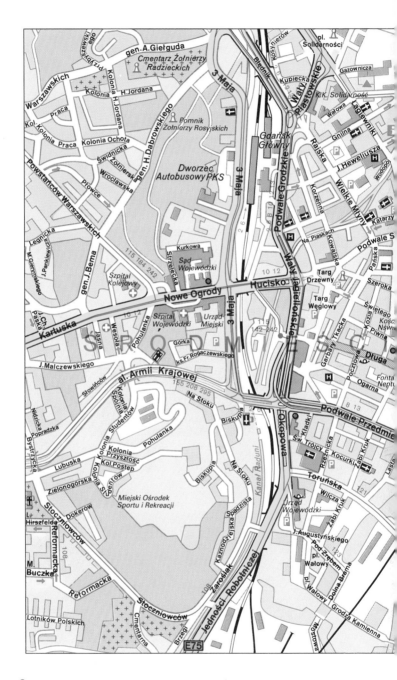
8

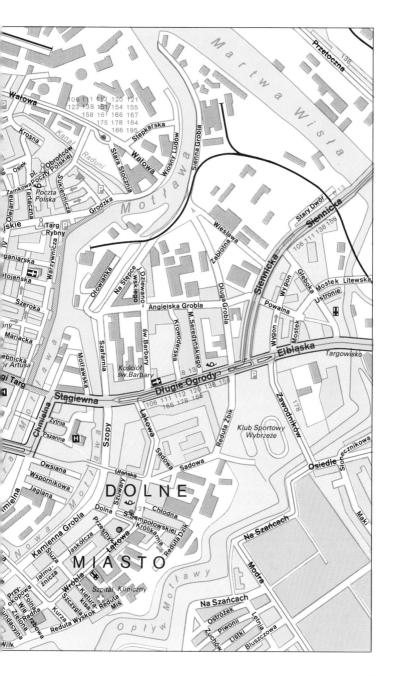

Above: The Gdańsk coat of arms in the Red Room.
Page 2: The Neptune Fountain on the Long Market.
Pages 6/7: The Church of Our Lady with the Old City in the background.

Town History

Gdańsk stands out among the several dozen historical towns of the Baltic sea coast. Its distinctness is the effect not so much of the thousand years of its existence, as of the dramatic nature of its history. Generations of its inhabitants have accumulated wealth for themselves and the city, passing on their achievements to successors who multiplied them. But many were also frequently forced by history to defend their own existence, to bear the highest sacrifice in the defense of human rights, of the right to self-government, of the native city or the country itself, and to rebuild its ruins. It was here that the first gun shots of the Second World War were heard, which ended in agony for Gdańsk. The new settlers who came in 1945 took up the work of their predecessors – the continuation of a great history and of the city's culture. Settlement in the area of today's Gdańsk can be traced back to the earlier Stone Age, to about 2,500 years B.C. From later periods several dozen sites of Eastern Pomeranian culture (500-400 B.C.) have been found, which indicates that there must have been considerable development of this settlement. Of the Roman Age, from the beginning of our era, there are findings connected with the old amber trail. Merchants used to travel over it from the south of Europe in search of the »Baltic gold«. Arabian coins from the 8th/9th centuries, found in such places as Św. Wojciech, are evidence that this trade route was attractive even after the fall of the Roman Empire.

The settlement easily became a permanent one because of the favorable conditions created at the mouth of the Vistula River, the largest Polish river, as it enters the sea. With its source in the mountains of southern Poland, the river has marked a natural transportation route for centuries. At the foot of the Wysoczyzna Gdańska/Gdańsk Upland, the river flows into the Baltic, taking in the waters of the Motława River in the last kilometers. It was here, at the mouth of the Motława, that the wetland formed a natural defense, although some of the settlements were established in Wysoczyzna. Settlements of the future Gdańsk were raised at a certain distance from the sea coast, which acted as protection against sea and ice. In the 9th century, in the region of today's

11

The Beautiful Madonna.

Długi Targ/Long Market, there was a fishing-farming-craftsmen's settlement. Investigations conducted after 1945 identified within the region of Zamczysko (between the streets Rycerska, Grodzka and Sukiennicza) a developed town, surrounded by an earth-and-wood embankment 20 m wide at the base, built in the 870s. Inside, separated by another embankment, was the seat of the local ruler and his staff, the remaining part was occupied by a fishing-craftsmen's settlement. Relics have been identified of a port on the Motława River.

In 997 Bishop Wojciech Sławnikowic of Prague came to this town, sent by the Polish ruler Boleslaw Chrobry to baptize »a considerable multitude of people« and to proceed on his missionary journey to the Prussian lands, where he died a martyr's death. Gdańsk is first mentioned in Latin transcription in 999 as Gyddanyzc in the Roman work »Vita Sancti Adalberti« (»The Life of St. Adalbert«). In the 1148 bull of Pope Eugenius III »castrum Kdanzk in Pomerania« (the castle Gdańsk in Pomerania) is mentioned.

Apart from St. Wojciech, another historically confirmed person of Gdańsk is Sambor, known as »the Prince of Pomeranians«, who in 1186 brought a Cistercian convent to Oliwa from the west-Pomeranian Kołbacz. In 1227 Prince Świetopełk II brought a Dominican convent from Cracow and handed over to them the Church of St. Nicholas. By that time there existed a settlement founded on Lübeck law, with a governor, Andrzej, and inhabitants descended from Lübeck, located most probably in the area of the later Długi Targ.

The area of today's Old Town, around the Parish Church of St. Catherine, was inhabited by people of Slavic origin, their governor being mentioned in 1253. The earliest document of the town registry office is from 1299.

In 1306 King Władysław Łokietek came to Gdańsk, in his effort to bring order to the administration procedures in a region so far from the capital Cracow. It seems that his measures were not very

The Grand Mill and the tower of the Church of St. Catherine.

successful, because in 1308 the Brandenburg army arrived, summoned by a Gdańsk palatine, to which the Gdańsk castellan replied by summoning the Teutonic Knights to help him. The Knights took Gdańsk, but slaughtered a portion of its Slavic inhabitants and a detachment of Polish knights, burning down the town.

The Teutonic Order took over the stronghold and in around 1340 completed the construction of a brick castle here. Another significant undertaking by the Teutonic Knights was to conduct a canal from the vicinity of Pruszcz along the Radunia River (1310-38), which drove the wheels of mills in the neighborhood of the Gdańsk

13

Church of St. Catherine. The river flows through the Old Town to this day, only the mills are not working any longer.

In 1342/43 Grand Master Rudolf König implemented legal regulations for the settlement area around the present Długi Targ, while his successor conferred the law of Chełmno in 1346. The document demarcated the town limits and determined the street layout. It defined the duty of raising fortification walls and made legal the town authorities. Full self-government rights were conferred by the charter of Grand Master Winrich von Kniprode in 1378. Dating from the beginning of the 15th century, the area known as the Rechtsstadt, or Urbs Principalis in Latin, occupied 42 hectares (about 100 acres). In Polish the name Główne Miasto, or the Main City, was adopted. Arrivals from the western countries, mostly German-speaking, settled here. A year earlier, in 1377, the Old Town had obtained its foundation charter, which was also no doubt an act confirming an existing status, since the office of mayor and a council had already been functioning here. Beyond the ramparts, in Osiek, which was a separate unit with its own authorities, lived Slavic and Prussian people of the old fishing settlement of the oldest Gdańsk. The Order increased the number of independent town units in 1380 by charters that founded the Młode Miasto/Young Town and the Stare Przedmiescie/Old Suburb. These were most probably efforts to create competing units that would weaken the development of the Main City, which as it grew tried to acquire independence from the strong Teutonic power. The conflicts kept mounting. Following the battle of Grunwald (1410), which ended in victory for Poland, the burghers of the Main City paid homage to the representative of King Władyslaw Jagiełło in Długi Targ. In revenge, in the next year the Teutonic Knights murdered the delegation that came to the castle. After a subsequent revolt against the Teutonic Order in 1416, the court of the Order had 18 burghers beheaded and confiscated their property, and the town was obligated to pay an immense tribute. At that time, i.e. at the beginning of the 15th century, Gdańsk had 20,000 inhabitants.

In 1440 Gdańsk signed a document establishing the Prussian Union, whose objective was to gain the independence of the Prussian towns and lands. In 1454 the people of Gdańsk destroyed the Teutonic castle, an event which marked the beginning of a thirteen-year war with the Order, to a large extent financed by Gdańsk.

King Kazimierz Jagiellończyk not only incorporated Gdańsk into the Kingdom of Poland again, but by a series of privileges in

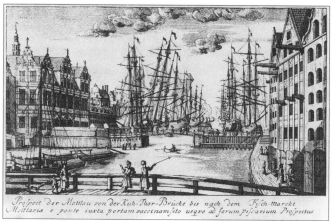

View of the Motława. Engraving by M. Deisch, 1765.

the years 1454-77 expanded the town's property by adding on
neighboring territory, and guaranteed Gdańsk the monopoly on the
entire sea trade of Poland. The monarch added splendor to the
Teutonic town coat of arms – crosses against a red background –
by adding the royal crown. The Main City also obtained consent
for the elimination of the Young Town, while the Old Town and
Osiek, independent until then, were subordinated to the council of
the Main City. Such a favorable arrangement, obtained as a result
of the thirteen-year war, was from then on defended by Gdańsk
against everyone, including the Kingdom of Poland.

The foundation charter of 1346 hastened the urbanization
process. Brick fortification walls still enclosed the town's houses
in the 14th century, and the number of tower-gates was over thirty.
The idea of the planned layout was to mark out the main directions
of the streets on the west-east axis, towards the port. From the side
of the water, too, each street was closed off by a gate, of which the
best preserved is the Chlebnicka Gate (first half of the 15th
century). It is thought that ships came to the wharfs by the gates;
here they were loaded and unloaded, and the port fees and customs
duties were collected. It is not certain whether any fortification
walls were built between the gates by the water. The largest gate on
the Motława is the Żuraw/Crane, which closes ulica Szeroka and
was raised in 1442-44 against the will of the Gdańsk Commander;
for a long time it has been regarded as the symbol of maritime
Gdańsk. It is an unusual example of medieval port techniques.

Portal of the Main Town Hall.

Simultaneously with the fortification walls, the town hall was built, possibly on the foundations of an older building. It was located on the main street, ulica Długa, in the neighborhood of Długi Targ – the most splendid square of medieval Gdańsk. Grounds were demarcated for the construction of the Parish Church of Our Lady. Work was taken up on the expansion of the Church of St. Nicholas. Other churches were built, beyond the Main City as well. The houses were usually of a frame construction, only the side walls were of brick, in compliance with the fire-safety regulations. In the 15th century the wealthiest merchants built facades of brick, or raised entire houses of brick. Wyspa Spichrzów/Granary Island, situated on the other side of the river, consisted solely of storage buildings. Until the end of the war with the Order (the Toruń Peace of 1466), the Gdańsk inhabitants with great labor rebuilt the town and strengthened it, fighting for their rights and bearing the cost of the domination by the Teutonic Order.

16

The Red Room of the Main Town Hall.

The end of the Thirteen Years' War marked the beginning of what is now known as the Golden Age of Gdańsk. On the one hand, the burdensome domination by the Teutonic Order was over, on the other hand there was incorporation into Poland (1454) again. Instead of the Gdańsk Commander, the burgrave had the sovereign rule, appointed by the king from among the notables of Gdańsk and representing him. Gdańsk defended its own social structures and its position in the Kingdom of Poland and later in the Republic of Poland resolutely and ably. The perpetual shortages of the Crown Treasury made it possible for the Gdańsk mayors to maintain their position and in addition abated conflicts. History recalls numerous examples of loans extended to the Polish Treasury. The town's revenue, guaranteed by the privileges granted by Kazimierz Jagiellończyk, was renegotiated and reconfirmed many times by his successors. Gdańsk was able to strengthen its position and power only through permanent ties with the Republic.

Ceiling panorama in the Main Town Hall, by van den Blocke, 1608.

The Court of Artus. Engraving by J.C. Schultz, mid-19th cent.

An important guarantee for Gdańsk's strong position was its membership in the Hanseatic League of towns, from the very beginning of its establishment in 1361. This international association of German mercantile towns made it possible not only to use the Hanseatic trading houses in Bruges, Bergen, London or Novgorod, but also facilitated banking operations, opened new doors, and alleviated customs and port duties. But in the Hanseatic League the Gdańsk merchants often faced problems, too, when resolutely defending their interests. When at the Hansa convention in 1498 an attempt was made to renew the principle of granting citizenship in Hanseatic towns only to German-speaking people, Gdańsk and the Prussian towns refused to comply on account of their subjection to the Polish Crown. Delegates from Gdańsk participated in Hansa conventions until 1669.

The era of prosperity began in the second half of the 15th century, first of all with the expansion of the city's fortification system and with the raising of the town hall tower, which until then had been forbidden by the Teutonic Commander. The Court of Artus was built, construction work was completed on the biggest Gothic church on the Baltic coast, the Parish Church of Our Lady. Secular and sacral interiors were created and eminent artists were invited from the west. In 1518 the Reformation began and with it

The Lions' Palace. Engraving by J.C. Schultz, mid-19th cent.

social unrest. Zygmunt I, like most Polish kings, received his homage at Długi Targ and in 1526 issued statutes that made the city system somewhat more democratic. This, however, did not change the fact that decisive authority was held by the patriciate.

Apart from the burgher guilds' donations of works of art for the church and secular interiors, it was outstanding representatives of the patriciate above all who commissioned paintings, brought over architects, builders, painters and sculptors from Augsburg, Dresden, Antwerp or Mechelen. Works by fine artists filled out the interiors of the Main City Hall, the Court of Artus and many churches. Ulica Długa together with Długi Targ, known as the Royal Way, were embellished by the facades of houses of the patriciate. These had classical Renaissance or Dutch mannerism forms and were richly decorated with stone details, bas-reliefs or fully sculptured figures. Here it must be said that all stone material was imported, and for example in the palace construction of Zielona Brama/Green Gate, designed by Hans Kramer of Dresden, the characteristic small-sized bricks, called Dutch bricks here, were imported from the Netherlands itself. The magnificence and architectural taste of Gdańsk was materially supported by its economic activity. For example, in 1583, 2,229 ships entered Gdańsk, mostly from the Netherlands. Arrivals from Flanders

21

included the van den Block family of famous sculptors and Hans Vredeman de Vries, creator of the design of the Sala Czerwona/Red Room of the Main City Hall. In front of the houses there appeared decorative porch slabs carved out of stone. They covered the cellar entrances and on the terraces of the porches social gatherings also took place. These porches are also known from other Hanseatic towns, such as Lübeck. Nowhere else, however, was there such a multitude of them, such a variety and wealth of decorative forms and multi-figure scenes carved into the front stones. From the Middle Ages on and until the end of the 18th century (the classicist period) they usually ornamented main streets.

The 16th century was not only a period of cultural and artistic growth. In 1568 the city went into open conflict with the Republic. As a measure against the growth of the war fleet of Zygmunt August, the last of the Jagiellon dynasty, 11 privateers of the royal ship were beheaded, following accusations of piracy. The privateer ships attempting to take refuge from a storm in the port, were fired at from the guns of the fortress defending the mouth of the Vistula River. The royal commission came across the blackened heads of the privateers at the Brama Wyżynna/High Gate. The king's death interrupted the commission's proceedings, and the aforementioned political skills of the Gdańsk councillors defused the conflict. When Stefan Batory, Prince of Transylvania, was elected King of Poland instead of the Habsburg pretender supported by Gdańsk, the council closed the gates and rolled out the cannons on the embankment. The Crown forces did not capture the town. The parliamentarians of Gdańsk, on the other hand, were successful, but only after dramatic and long negotiations.

It would be a mistake to assume that this was an attempt to break off the ties with Poland which constituted the economic base of the city's welfare. Proof of loyalty to the Republic was given by Gdańsk in the wars of succession with Sweden. In 1626 the victorious army of Gustavus Adolfus Vasa, unsuccessfully attacking the fortifications of territory belonging to Gdańsk, was unable to extort a neutrality agreement from the council. In the same year King Zygmunt III Waza came here and established the Gdańsk Commission of Royal Warships, which prepared warships for battle with Sweden. When war came to Poland, the Gdańsk forces aided the royal forces in the battle for nearby Puck. The war was not over till 1629. During the second Northern War, which ended with the Peace in Oliwa in 1660 Gdańsk rejected proposals of proclaiming neutrality, in spite of the blockade of the port and

The Churn Gate.

the siege by Swedish forces. To end this historical account, it is also worth recalling another significant event. For six months at the turn of 1733 and 1734, Gdańsk sheltered within its walls the Polish King Stanislaw Leszczyński during the siege by the Russian army and held out until the day when the unfortunate monarch fled by ship in disguise, leaving the country in the hands of August III of Saxony. Gdańsk was to pay a contribution of one million thalers to Anna, Empress of Russia. The present for the new ruler was much more modest.

Putting aside the course of world history for a while, it is worth coming back to the history of the city itself and the magnificent growth in art, culture and science. Modern architectural forms became the rule in the Gdańsk of the 16th century, which was undergoing reconstruction and modernization. The buildings designed by the aforementioned builder Kramer include two

Epitaph of Eduard Blemke in the Church of Our Lady.

houses in the tradition of the Italian theoretician Serlio: the Lions'
Castle and the English House. In 1564-68 the Brama Zielona/
Green Gate, appropriated for the palace of the Polish kings, also of
his design, but built by Regnier of Amsterdam, decorated Długi
Targ on the water side. This was the first monumental work repre-
senting the forms of Dutch mannerism. Antoni van Obberghen of
Flanders built the Town Hall of the Old Town (1586-88) and the
Grand Armory (1602-05), the most Flemish structures of the city.
The Brama Złota/Golden Gate, the work of Abraham van den
Blocke (1612-14), accentuates the opening of the ulica Długa with
classicist forms, while the facade of the Złota Kamienica/Golden
House at Długi Targ, one of the finest creations by this artist, is
unique in that it is completely covered with stone reliefs of
historical themes. The Gdańsk guild of sculptors and stone masons

24

The organ in the Church of Our Lady.

was a very strong organization. From this group came Andreas Schlüter the Younger, creator of many facades, particularly known for his work on the facade of the Royal Chapel (1678-81) and the sculptures of the Berlin Armory. The fine works of later sculptors, including J. H. Meissner, still ornament the porches of many Gdańsk houses. During the 16th and 17th centuries, many works by Gdańsk sculptors were sent abroad – to Sweden, Denmark, Transylvania, and also into the interior of the Republic.

The medieval brick fortification walls were becoming a weaker and weaker defense for the city in the era of the development of artillery. In the second half of the 16th century, on the western side, the most exposed to attack, high earth embankments were begun and deep and broad moats were dug, strengthened with bastions. In 1588, above the green curtain of the embankment there appeared the stone mass of the Brama Wyżynna/High Gate – the main entrance into Gdańsk. The whole of the city was surrounded by a system of embankments and moats, designed by Van den Bosch of Holland and built under his supervision in 1619-36. Within these lived about 70,000 people at the time. The new fortification system ensured safety until 1793, when Gdańsk fell to Prussia in the third division of Poland.

The paintings preserved in Gdańsk are largely imports from the southern German countries and the Netherlands. But Gdańsk artists also contributed many fine works of art, especially at the end of the 16th and in the 17th century. The Gdańsk painters' guild was established in the 17th century. Antoni Moeller, the earliest of the esteemed Gdańsk painters, creator of the superbly painted panoramic views of the city and Długi Targ, also left behind a series of religious, allegorical works and portraits. Bartlomiej Strobel, Andnrzej Stech, Daniel Schultz and Herman Han were outstanding painters of the 17th century. Their paintings decorate the gallery of the National Museum in Gdańsk and also churches in the city center and in Oliwa. An outstanding graphic artist permanently resident in Gdańsk was Wilhelm Hondius from Holland (1601-52), a popular portrait-painter of royal families. It is possible that out of his studio came Jeremiasz Falck (1609-77), who added Polonus to his name, and who was known for numerous works in Paris, Stockholm and Holland. Daniel Mikołaj Chodowiecki (1706-1801), a well-known painter and graphic artist, although born in Gdańsk, spent most of his life in Berlin. His »Diary of a Journey to Gdańsk« and sketches published in the album of this journey in 1773, paint a penetrating and at the same time warm picture of the city and its inhabitants.

The Royal Chapel.

The wealthy furnishings of Gdańsk homes are known mainly from engravings, descriptions and the few examples of collections, as they shared the fate of the city at the end of the last war. Many of the characteristic Gdańsk wardrobes have been preserved, the huge items having been made specially for the splendid vestibules of houses, courts and palaces. They were usually from the 18th century, richly sculpted and with marquetry. The tradition of Gdańsk furniture for the splendid interiors lasted until the end of the 19th century. Wood carving, dating back to medieval times in its tradition, flourished in the 16th and 17th centuries, the best examples being the decorations of the Main City Hall and the Court of Artus. An equally high artistic level is represented by baroque works – the grand organs of the cathedral in Oliwa and of the churches of Our Lady and St. Nicholas, as well as numerous church or household furnishings, richly sculpted, painted and gilded. In the 17th century considerable achievements were

The vestibule of the Main Town Hall.

attained in artistic smithery. Particularly well known was the grating, plaited when still hot. Gdańsk was also famous for items cast in bronze. These included church and secular candlesticks or chandeliers, medals and other objects. From the beginning of the 17th century Gdańsk goldsmith products had no equal, not only on territories of the Republic. The description »Gdańsk workmanship« brought a certain standing to the owners of this silverware or tinware.

The founding of the Gdańsk Gymnasium in 1558 stimulated the development of the Gdańsk world of science. The Gymnasium was located in the building of the old Franciscan monastery (today the National Museum). In the 17th century the school, known at the time as the Baltic Athenaeum, reached the highest point in its development. Its graduates were admitted to the third year of university studies. The school was famous for its natural and medical sciences. The humanities and Protestant theology were

Johann Hevelius. Epitaph in the Church of St. Catherine.

also well developed. It was here that in 1613 Joachim Oelhaf performed the first public autopsy in Central Europe, and in 1635 Daniel Schwabe carried out the first ever successful operation on the stomach. The potential of the Gdańsk medical environment is also testified to by the establishment of the Collegium Medicum in 1614. This was a kind of Chamber of Physicians, the first in Europe, which was granted a privilege by the Polish King Władyslaw IV Waza in 1636. From 1589 on Polish was also taught as a subject. The first lecturer was the poet Jan Rybinski, the last of the twenty-two lecturers was Krzysztof Celestyn Mrongowiusz, author of numerous textbooks for teaching the Polish language. The Gymnasium's book collection is kept in the Gdańsk Library of the Polish Academy of Sciences at ul. Wałowa 15.

At least two scientists born in Gdańsk made a permanent contribution to world science. In 1611, in the respectable family of the brewer Hewelke, a son called Jan was born. After completing the

Academic Gymnasium he continued his studies abroad, completing them in Leiden. He was particularly interested in astronomy and devoted the rest of his life to it. He printed the results of his observations in the outstanding Gdańsk printing houses, using the Latin version of his name – Hevelius, hence the Polish name Heweliusz. He was the first Gdańsk citizen to obtain honorary membership in the Royal Society of London (1644). To his city he dedicated the work »Selenographia« in 1647, the fruit of long studies of the moon. A year before his death, in 1687, Daniel Gabriel Fahrenheit, who developed the thermometer scale still in use, was born in Gdańsk. In the same year the printed work »Beschreibung der Stadt Danzig durch Reinhold Curicken Secretarium« appeared, written earlier (1645) by a secretary of the town council. The work fully deserves to be called scientific; with numerous footnotes, illustrations of buildings of those days, descriptions of the most interesting interiors, the city history and its system, it is today a valuable source of information for historians dealing with Gdańsk.

The first of Gdańsk's scientific societies, the Literary Society, was established in 1720. Of particular significance was the activity of the Natural Science Society, established by Daniel Gralath in 1743. The Society conducted fundamental studies and published the results. From the Gdańsk circle of scientists came the proposal to establish a national royal scientific society, which did not gain the approval of Augustus III of Saxony. However, his successor, Stanislaw August Poniatowski, the last Polish king, was a member of the Society.

The crisis of the Polish state in the second half of the 18th century affected Gdańsk as well. After the first division of Poland, the city still remained in the Republic, but lost large suburban areas, Żuławy and the Hel Peninsula, to Prussia. The reserve manifested towards the Prussians, in the fear of absolutist despotism, evoked the reaction of King Frederick II. From the year 1772 on (the first division), an economic blockade was imposed. The new tariffs and the inhibition of trade on the Vistula lowered the city's revenue. Joanna Schopenhauer, a citizen of Gdańsk and mother of the famous philosopher, wrote: »Over the years we all felt the yoke of foreign rule more and more and this had an increasingly devastating effect on the old prosperity of my unfortunate home town...«. In 1793 Gdańsk was taken by the Prussian army, which overcame the resistance of the masses.

Gdańsk became a free city for the first time in 1807, following the Peace of Tilsit. However, after the return of Napoleon from

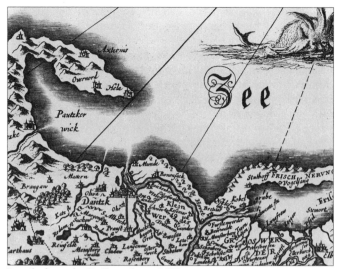

Detail of map by K. Henneberg, 1635.

Moscow in 1813, a ring of Prussian and Russian armies closed off the city, which surrendered after a siege that lasted a year. Over 1,000 houses were seriously damaged, the buildings of Granary Island were burned down. In spite of a serious limitation of trade, which was the effect of the border cordons in the upper course of the Vistula River, the city continued to develop. Its position, however, was no longer as strong as it used to be. But economic development, the considerable influx of people and the growth of industry brought with them progress. In 1852 Gdańsk was linked to the Prussian railway system, and in 1862 the city already had a connection to Warsaw.

In accordance with tradition, the shipbuilding industry continued to develop. Next to the Klawitter shipyard, which dates from the eighteenth century, the Royal (and later the Emperor's) Shipyard was built as well as Schichau's shipyard – a branch of the Elbląg establishment. As early as 1840 the construction of iron ships began and it should be emphasized that this was a modern industry. At the beginning of the 20th century the Emperor's Shipyard was employing three thousand people. Shipyards and the accompanying metal industry provided great possibilities for employment. A considerable development of the processing industry also took place.

31

As a result of the influx of newcomers and the expansion of the city limits, the number of inhabitants increased considerably. While there were fewer than 40,000 at the end of the 18th century, in 1914 there were already 175,000 inhabitants, and the garrison numbered 20,000 soldiers. The proportion of Polish people clearly decreased; at the beginning of the 19th century they accounted for about 30% of the population. The first secular union of Poles, Ogniwo, was established in 1876.

The period of division lasted from 1815 to 1919. The Free City of Gdańsk came into being in the year 1919 on account of the Treaty of Versailles, stretching over an area of 1,900 square kilometers, with a population of about 400,000 inhabitants. The League of Nations supervised the observance of this status through its High Commissioner. The Polish issues were represented by the General Commissioner of the Republic of Poland. In practice, executive power was vested in the city Senate, and legislative power in the Seym (Volkstag). The Council of Ports and Waterways in Gdańsk, comprised of representatives of Gdańsk and the Republic of Poland, held surveillance over the sea area of the Free City of Gdańsk.

Interrelations between nationality groups became complicated for many reasons. They were the consequence of mutual distrust felt for various reasons, as well as of unemployment. After 1933, in accordance with the Nazi slogan »Zurück zum Reich« (back to the Reich) strong hostility grew, fueled by Gauleiter Albert Forster, posted in Gdańsk by Adolf Hitler. In 1920, the Polish minority still held seven of the 120 seats in the Seym, but in 1935 only two of the 72 seats, of which 38 were held by the National-Socialist Party. In 1934 K.A. Greiser became President of the Senate, clearly representing NSDAP policies. The Polish community, the Union of Poles, in the Free City of Gdańsk had 11,499 members in March 1938. From 1922 on the Polish Gymnasium functioned with a background support of 26 elementary schools and day-nurseries. At the Gdańsk Polytechnic 30% of the students were Polish. In the Free City, 98 Polish cultural and vocational organizations were operating. There was the Union of Polish Scouts, the »Sókoł« Gymnastics Society, the choirs »Lutnia« and the choir of St. Cecilia. Several periodicals were published, especially the »Gazeta Gdańska« (from 1891). The cultural, scientific and sport life of German Gdańsk also thrived. The traditionally good relationship between the two nationalities was maintained, but from 1933 on life became harder for the Gdańsk Poles.

Court of Artus and Neptune Fountain in the 1930s.

The first gun shots of the Second World War were fired on September 1st, 1939, at 4:45, by the German battleship Schleswig-Holstein. They fell on the grounds of the Polish Military Transit Depot on the Westerplatte Peninsula, which was defended by 182 soldiers and officers armed with infantry weapons and three cannons. After seven days of fighting they surrendered. The resistance of the civil forces of the Polish Post Office lasted for nearly a day. A month later, 39 of the postal employees were executed; their remains were found much later, in 1991. Among them was Franciszek Krause, the Kashubian relation on the mother's side of Günter Grass, the outstanding German writer, who was born in 1927 in the Gdańsk district of Wrzeszcz. In 1939-44 fate was kinder to Gdańsk, sparing it intensive air-raids (apart from the attacks on the port and the shipbuilding industry). But it was not kind to the Poles; the first transport of Poles left for the concentration camp in nearby Sztutowo on September 2nd, 1939. Chances of survival were minimal for activists of Polish organizations and Catholic priests.

At the beginning of 1945 the fortified region of Gdańsk, Sopot and Gdynia was defended by 15 divisions of the Wehrmacht, 3 armored divisions and other units. Gdańsk was flooded with masses of fugitives from the eastern territories. After the Soviet army took Sopot and Gdynia, the struggles continued in Gdańsk. They came to a halt on March 29. A day later the German forces

Town panorama around 1680.

surrendered, withdrawing to the region of Westerplatte. On March 30, 1945, the Polish Gdańsk voivodship was established.

The devastation of the city center was estimated at 90%, of the suburbs at 60%. The scale of destruction of the historical part of Gdańsk was to a large extent determined by the wooden construction of the roofs and the rafter framing. In the conditions of siege, and then of street fighting, fires spread with ease. The establishment of a voivodship of Gdańsk was regarded as natural, and the reconstruction of the city as necessary. In the 19th century, and especially after gaining independence in 1918, Gdańsk was associated in the minds of the Poles with the notion of »the old sea capital of Poland«. This concept was strengthened by the construction between the wars of Gdynia and its modern port, the largest on the Baltic. It was imperative to restore Gdańsk back to life. Undoubtedly, the symbolism of the place also had an

34

influence on the decision of reconstruction: it was here that the war began which devastated the country and cost the life of every fifth inhabitant.

In 1946 work was begun on the general layout of the city. In the first drafts there were plans for a city of commerce and administration. Later it was decided to make the old city center a residential area. The historical value of many destroyed monumental structures made reconstruction a valid option. An important factor was that many stone details had been preserved, often of a high artistic value. Reconstruction was possible on the old foundations and preserved facilities could still be used, which lowered the costs of the undertaking. The government resolution of 1952 approved the reconstruction of the entire Main City area. There was no point in fully reconstructing all the houses preserved until 1945. There were detailed plans to solve various issues: the insides of the old structures in courtyards and outbuildings were not reconstructed; the lenght of reconstructed houses was lessened to ensure that daylight reached all interiors; only facades with historically documented appearances were reconstructed. Also, a dozen or so of the historically most valuable houses were chosen for reconstruction together with their original interiors.

Large teams of research workers and designers prepared working drafts from the beginning of the 1950s on; their work lasted for over a decade. At the same time, work was started on the reconstruction of the Main City beginning with ulica Ogarna. As the work progressed, all those participating in the great reconstruction continually reached new heights of perfection. This is the only example in Europe of the reconstruction of a destroyed historical city on such a large area – 42 hectares (about 100 acres). The best workmanship of this complete rebuilding of a city turned out to be on ulica Mariacka, where all the porches were reconstructed.

But the main problem after 1945 was to provide shelter and jobs for the people arriving in the devastated city. The first hard years were filled with removing the rubble, reconstructing and repairing the port, the shipyard and nearly all the industrial establishments. At the same time, all the municipal services and schools had to be reorganized from the beginning. Two schools of higher education that existed before the war were reopened and new ones were established as the need arose. In 1970 the University of Gdańsk was established, the sixth college of higher education.

The urban development of Gdańsk was closely connected to the structure of the neighboring coastal towns Sopot and Gdynia, now no longer separated by a border. The term »Trojmiasto« (Tri-City) has been used from the beginning of the 1950s, although each of the cities is a separate unit in itself, with its own municipal administration. The municipal railway system resolved the initial transportation problems, but these problems still remain, in spite of building a ring road for the transit traffic. Gdańsk has expanded its area to 260 square kilometers (160 square miles), while the number of inhabitants is approaching one million. The buildings of new housing districts are filling up the vacant areas of the narrow coastal strip. Areas of the Wysoczyzna Gdańska/Gdańsk Upland were developed for the building of satellite towns. The wooded suburban areas on the Wyżyna/Highland have been preserved, creating the Tri-City Landscape Park.

The main economic and social issue at present is the restructuring of a part of the port of Gdańsk and of houses on

Part of the Monument to the Killed Shipyard Workers, 1980.

Granary Island. This is a grand project that awaits investors, similarly to the unfinished construction of the North Port.

However, the most important task in Gdańsk during the last half-century was the gradual revigorating of the ruined former trade imperium by new arrivals. They came from cities and villages far away from the sea, mainly from the areas annexed by the USSR in 1939, directed to the new land on the strength of the agreements of Yalta and Potsdam. People from the central and southern regions of the country also came, as well as from the traditional Gdańsk hinterland of Kashubia and Pomerania. They joined the few remaining Gdańsk inhabitants of Polish citizenship who had survived the war years. There was no certainty whether this great settlement movement would be successful.

Today, it can be said with full conviction that this process brought better results than expected. The second generation of Gdańsk inhabitants, born after 1945, identifies itself not only with its place of birth, but also with the tradition of its great history. Like former generations, they form a strong economic potential for the country, and provide a significant and expansive environment for art, the humanities and sciences open to the whole Baltic area. The Gdańsk culture radiates to the outside, enriching its ties with Scandinavia and its neighbors of the eastern and western coastal zone. It is enough to take a walk in the city, to look into the numerous art galleries, antique shops or artisan workshops, to sit down for a coffee or beer in one of the many cafes or restaurants, or to become lost in thought in the stately silence of the monumental hall of the Church of Our Lady, to reaffirm the conviction that the thousand-year history of Gdańsk has not been interrupted.

An important attribute of the people of Gdańsk continues to be their strong bond with the city and the sea, their pride in their achievements and the belief that it is possible to do and have much more. The esteem for individual and collective human rights characteristic for this city, the readiness to defend these, were expressed in the dramatic events of December 1970. People of Gdańsk died on the streets of their city, which they had rebuilt themselves. They perished at the gate to the shipyard, which was the starting-point and center of the fight for human dignity and national independence. It was from here that the electrician from the Gdańsk shipyard, Lech Wałesa, started his path as the workers' leader of »Solidarity«, the free trade union and socio-political movement. It was from here that, supported by his compatriots, he attained the office of President of the Republic of Poland. These

Strike in the Gdańsk-Shipyard.

facts also make it possible to state that the great labor of post-war reconstruction, of creating a society that is new, but firmly embedded in Gdańsk tradition, has borne exceptional fruits.

The Union of Baltic Towns was founded in Gdańsk on September 20th 1991 by delegations from 44 towns.

The historic Green Gate, built in 1564-68 to serve as residence for the visiting polish kings, houses the permanent secretariate of this organization.

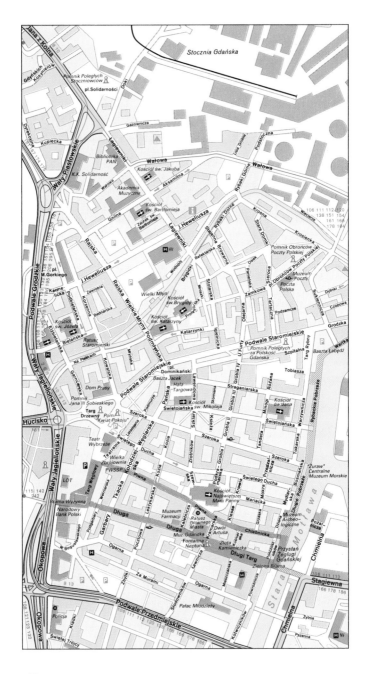

40

Walk
The Main City

The Brama Wyżynna/Upland Gate • Ante-gate of ul. Długa. • The Brama Złota/Golden Gate • The House of the Confraternity of St. George • Ulica Długa • The Main City Hall. • The Długi Targ/Long Market • Neptune's Fountain • Dwór Artusa/The Court of Artus. • The Złota Kamienica/Golden House • The Brama Zielona/Green Gate • The Chlebnicka Gate • Ulica Chlebnicka The Church of Our Lady • Ulica Piwna Wielka Zbrojownia/The Great Armory

The Main City (Głowne Miasto) is the center of historical Gdańsk. In 1346 the inhabitants of the settlements that had been established much earlier obtained city rights. On an area of 42 hectares (about 104 acres) they raised a powerful, wealthy city, expressing the pride they felt for their economic achievements and success by financing the construction of buildings, works of art, and book collections. A considerable portion of this heritage survived up to March 1945. Their successors came here from afar, immediately after the complete destruction of the city and by 1950 they had removed from here two million cubic meters of rubble. They protected the preserved wall fragments and stone decoration pieces, which they had carefully sorted out from among the ruins in order to use them for the later reconstruction. They reconstructed the city out of respect for the history of this piece of Europe and the generations who had created it. They furnished the rebuilt interiors of churches and secular houses with original works of art which had been prudently taken out of the city in the 1940s by Gdańsk curators in an effort to save them from destruction. This was how the unplanned international cooperation of two consecutive generations of Gdańsk inhabitants came about.

The **Brama Wyżynna/Upland Gate** opens the Royal Way which extends all the way to the Motława River. Willem van den Blocke, the outstanding Flemish sculptor from Mechelen who had

The route of the walk is marked in grey in the map opposite.

41

settled permanently in Gdańsk, designed the gate's stone decoration. The model was the St. George's Gate in Antwerp and the architectural pattern-book published in 1577 by Hans Vredeman de Vries. The work was carried out in the years 1586-88, enriching the city with a structure of architectural and decorative forms that were very modern for those times. The classical rustic work of the main facade, extending to the cornice, stands in contrast to the rich frieze decorated with the arms of Royal Prussia, Poland and Gdańsk – a very popular theme in Gdańsk art of the modern age. The eagle of the emblem of the Republic has on its breast the Young Bull of Stanislaw August Poniatowski, the last king of Poland. One of the Latin sayings carved out under the cornice is: »Peace, freedom and unity are the greatest values of a state«. Until 1895 the Gate was built into ground fortifications, and the deep and wide moat dug out in front of it was filled with water. To enter the city you had to cross a wooden drawbridge. The back facade of the building obtained its decoration in 1884. In about 1900 a neo-Renaissance building housing a bank was raised on the right side of the Gate. Many splendid buildings were raised in this style at the turn of the century, referring to the times of the greatest splendor of Gdańsk.

The brick complex of the medieval **ante-gate of ulica Długa** consists of two houses: the Torture House reconstructed in 1593 by Anton van Obberghen of Flanders and the High Prison Tower, raised in height in 1508-09 by master builder Michal Enkinger. Until modern ground fortifications were built in the second half of the 16th century, the walls of the gate, which linked both houses, stood over a moat filled with water. The entrance to the city was also guarded by brick walls raised behind the moat, which are visible at the Targ Węglowy/Coal Market. Inside the Torture House and the Prison Tower, the Museum of the History of Gdańsk organizes exhibitions on the administration of justice and the former prison function of the two buildings.

The **Brama Złota/Golden Gate** adds splendor to the entrance to ulica Długa. The Renaissaince structure was designed by Abraham van den Blocke and built in 1612-14 by master builder Jan Strakowski. The stone sculptures of the attic, created in 1648 by Piotr Ringering, were removed in 1880 because of their poor state of preservation. Fortunately, the Gdańsk engraver Jeremiasz Falck Polonus had recorded them in his works, so that during the reconstruction work after 1950, the best sculptors of the city's School of Art had a model to follow when sculpting new ones. In the allegorical sculptures and inscriptions the ideal virtues of a

House facades in the Ulica Długa.

citizen are portrayed. On the front side there stand the figures of
Peace, Freedom, Wealth and Glory, while on the ulica Długa side
those of Prudence, Piety, Justice and Unity. The front inscription
reads: »May those fare well who love thee, may peace be in thy
walls, and good fortune in thy palaces«. On the opposite side:
»Through unity small states rise, through lack of it great states
fall«. With this ideological program Gdańsk greeted its visitors,
and these citizen virtues were recommended for its inhabitants.
The building adjacent to the Gate on the left side is the **House of
the Confraternity of St. George**, an exclusive confraternity of the
patriciate. Built in brick by Jerzy Glotau in 1487-94, it represents

late-Gothic forms. The metal figure of its patron saint which crowns the roof is a copy from the 1950s (the original is in the National Museum). The Association of Polish Architects has its seat here.

Ulica Długa, passing into Długi Targ, is part of a medieval trade route that led to a crossing over the Motława River. It was then already described as »Via regia«, or Royal Way. The name is justified by the fact that from the 15th century on the kings used to reside here during their numerous visits. Kazimierz Jagiellończyk began this tradition in 1454. The distinct curve of the street resulted from the necessity of subordinating the plan drawn up in 1343 to the already existing buildings. Even though after 1945 reconstruction was carried out with great care, on

Sundial on the Town Hall.

the basis of scientific historical studies, old drawings and photographs and with salvaged stone details being incorporated, the present appearance differs from the old one. The construction of a new bridge on the Motława River has made it possible to remove vehicle traffic from here. The old facades that had undergone reconstruction in the 19th or 20th century were rebuilt and restored. The porches, which had been in front of each house, were not rebuilt, these having already given way to the needs of traffic and commercial reconstruction of the ground floors in the 19th century. Though based on research and carried out with great care, this reconstruction is nevertheless a modern interpretation of the appearance of a historical street.

The house at No.12 was built in 1776 by Jan Beniamin Dreyer for Jan Uphagen, councillor and patrician. The facade is built in the style of the late baroque period, on the ground floor the high windows of the splendid vestibule, typical for Gdańsk houses of

44

Entrance to the Main Town Hall.

the time, have been recreated. Uphagen was a collector of works of art and furniture, and his successors continued this tradition. Fragments of interior furnishings have survived and a museum exhibition is to be organized here. This is one of the few houses that has been entirely reconstructed, with consideration for the original interior layout on each storey. Houses No. 71 and 74, on the opposite side of the street, have survived the war. In the course of their renovation, historical fragments of earlier brick facades were uncovered from beneath the plasterwork and restored. The houses at No. 69 and 70 are also original, with eclectic forms of facades from the turn of the 19th and 20th centuries. The house at No. 28, with a palace facade, raised in around 1560 for the famous Mayor Constantin Ferber, draws on Italian architectural forms, decorated with pilasters, busts and statues of ancient heroes. The house of Freder No. 29 (ab. 1625) is distinguished not only by its stone medallions of the busts of Roman emperors, but also by the sign »Pro invidia« (for jealousy) in the upper medallion. The house at No. 30, built in 1619 by the architect and sculptor Abraham van den Blocke, represents typical forms of Dutch mannerism. The original rich stone decorations contrasted with the brick facade. The house at No. 35 is the Lions' Castle, built in 1569 by master builder Hans Kramer of Dresden. The classical rhythm of the pilasters and the decreasing height of the storeys point to the influence of Sebastian Serlio, the theoretician of Italian Renaissance architecture. Here, too, the viewer will recognize the authentic stone elements, saved from the ruins, preserved and incorporated into the completely restored building. The house at No. 37, from 1563, was decorated by sculptors Henry Linth of Antwerp and Cornelius Brun from Brussels. The authentic fragments of the sculpture decorations are clearly different from the reconstructed fragments. The house at No. 45 was built in around 1560 for one of the wealthiest families of Gdańsk – the Conerts. They commissioned the construction of a family house resembling most closely the Italian Renaissance ideals, in order to impress others. Today, the seat of the Polish Association of Tourism and Local History (PTTK) is located here.

Faithful reconstruction of the facades of Gdańsk houses was not only possible thanks to old photographs. In the course of the designing work, three volumes of copperplate engravings by Jan Karol Schultz, issued in 1842-67, turned out to be an invaluable aid. Schultz, an outstanding graphic artist, painter and professor at the Gdańsk School of Fine Arts, created the Society for the Protection of Historical Monuments and contributed to the preservation of many houses in Gdańsk. A century later, his graphic work again turned out to be useful for the city he loved. One of the towers of the southern row of fortification walls that he was unable to save from dismantling in the 19th century, was given his name following post-war reconstruction.

There were already references to the **Main City Hall** in 1357, but they concerned the earlier building. The two lower storeys of today's main building were created in the years 1379-82. Only after the removal of the Teutonic Order from the city was it possible to raise the town hall by adding a third storey and to build a tower (1468-92). Also during this time a beautiful attic was created on the Długi Targ side, with distinct Flemish influences. In 1556 the master craftsman Dirk Daniels built a wooden copper-plated dome that crowned the tower, and at a height of 80 meters affixed a metal gilded statue of King Zygmunt August. Jan Moor of s'Hertogenbosch installed a carillon in the dome. The stone

View across the Main Town towards the harbor.

railing of the attic with the arms of Gdańsk, Poland and Royal Prussia dates from 1652. The three wings that form the present courtyard were completed in 1593-96. The 1945 fire burned out the interiors and the tower dome collapsed. In 1950, the restored figure of the king, taken from the rubble, once more stood at the top of the steel dome. In 1970 the Museum of the History of Gdańsk was opened. A visit to the town hall interior is a must when in Gdańsk. It is absolutely necessary to see the Sala Czerwona/Red Room, which is an authentic, outstanding example of Dutch mannerism, the exhibition on the destruction and reconstruction of Gdańsk, and the panoramic view of the city from the tower.

The entrance to the Town Hall from ulica Długa is by way of a splendid flight of stairs and a portal, created in 1766-68 by Daniel Eggert. The symmetry of the heraldic composition of a pair of lions holding a shield with the city coat of arms has been disturbed. One of the lions has his head turned away from the crest and it appears as if both lions were turned in the direction of the Brama Złota/Golden Gate. According to an old Gdańsk saying, they

47

turned their gaze in the direction from which the king used to arrive at the Town Hall, awaiting his majesty and his protection. The Town Hall was the most important place of the town community. To the left on the ground floor there was the sentry guardroom and opposite (on the present premises of the »Palowa« cafe) were the city scales. Here also were kept measurement gauges, and fees were collected. On the first floor is the Council Room, where decisions were made on the most important issues concerning the city, where delegations were received, and nearly all the Polish kings after Kazimierz Jagiellończyk resided. Aleksander (1504) and Zygmunt the Old (1526) stayed in the Town Hall, too. Other monarchs chose the houses at Długi Targ. On the opposite side is the Sala Ławy/Bench Room or court room. Its verdicts could be appealed against only to the king. Two small rooms called the Mały/Little and Wielki/Great Krzysztof served as a chapel and as archives for the council. Here important documents were kept – privileges, accounting books, land registries, small and big seals (the latter were used only for documents of the highest importance).

The splendid entrance-hall has lost its former furnishing. Only the Dutch ceramic tiles of the 17th century remain in the window niches. The finely sculptured wooden spiral stairs with baroque forms and the gallery are the work of contemporary artists, as are the paintings on the larch-wood ceiling, executed by J. Wnukowa. The original baroque portal of 1680, with the arms of Jan III Sobieski on the breast of an eagle, leads to the Wielka Sala Rady/Grand Council Room, also called the Czerwona Sala/Red Room. The interior furnishings, together with the portal and a pair of splendid doors were dismantled before 1945, and, following painstaking conservation, are now located in their original places. The design of the interior was executed by Hans Vredeman de Vries, an outstanding theoretician and master of Dutch mannerism who came here in 1592. In 1593-96 Szymon Herle of Gdańsk and his team made the wooden benches by the walls, the carved friezes with inlay and the decorative door. Willem van der Meer of Gandava is the creator of the fire-place (1593). The allegorical-historical paintings on the walls were done by de Vries himself (1595). The decorative ceiling with paintings by Isaac van den Blocke was created in 1611 (the wood-carving work was by Szymon Herle). Our attention is drawn to the oval painting on the ceiling, »Allegory of the Union of Gdańsk with the Republic«, framed by the finely carved arms of Poland, Gdańsk, Lithuania and Royal Prussia. The allegorical paintings on the ceiling portray

The Court of Artus and the Neptune Fountain.

historical and symbolical scenes, which the councillors were to emulate. With its completely preserved interior furnishings dating from a single era, this council chamber is a rarity in Europe. The neighboring room is the Mala Sala Rady/Small Council Room with paintings by H. Żuławska and tapestries by J. Wnukowa. After visiting the exhibition on the reconstruction of Gdańsk (one floor higher), it is a must to go up the tower. When the town hall was on fire in 1945, the temperature inside the tower was so high that the surface of the bricks softened and began to drip down. After managing the 102 stairs we find ourselves 48 meters above street level.

The view from the east is onto the **Długi Targ/Long Market** bordered by the Brama Zielona/Green Gate, and behind it the buildings of Granary Island. To the left of the Gate is the highest

The Golden House.

historical house, the Dom Angielski/English House. At Długi Targ, the area of the porches is clearly visible. The northern view to a large extent consists of the monumental Church of Our Lady. The buildings of the quarter situated to the right of the church (between the streets Chlebnicka and Mariacka) are a fine example of post-war reconstruction of Gdańsk. Between the rows of houses along the streets there are vast green recreational grounds. Only a few houses have been rebuilt in their original height, the remaining ones are lower. Until 1945, the currently vacant areas were heavily built-up. The western view is onto ulica Długa and the Brama

The Long Market.

Złota, behind which stands the Wieża Więzienna/Prison Tower. To the right are the picturesque gables of the Grand Armory and the light-colored building of the Wybrzeże Theater between the Targ Węglowy/Coal Market, and the Targ Drzewny/Lumber Market. The octagonal brick tower Jacek strengthens the corner of the medieval fortification walls of the Main City. To the right there begins the area of the Old Town. The tower and roofs of the Church of St. Catherine and the Wielki Młyn/ Great Mill can be seen, and also the building of the Hevelius Hotel and office buildings. Behind them is the outline of the cranes and halls of the

Gdańsk Shipyard. The south view illustrates the principle of reconstruction of the Stare Przedmiescie/Old Suburb, which is located beyond the Podwale Przedmiejskie route. On the right is the towerless Holy Trinity Church and next to it, in the former Franciscan monastery, the National Museum. On the left is the Church of SS Peter and Paul.

At Długi Targ/Long Market there stands **Neptune's Fountain**, created in 1606-13. The statue of the king of the seas is the work of foundryman Piotr Husen, the pool of the fountain and the bowl have been modernized many times. The house at No. 2, on the other side of Długi Targ, together with the corner house at ul. Ławnicza and several neighboring houses, is one of the so-called royal houses that frequently housed the kings with their closest attendants. On the porch there is an original stone slab with the date 1577, the only example from the 16th century. The finely reconstructed metal grating of the porch testifies to the high level of contemporary Gdańsk smithery.

The **Court of Artus** was built in 1476-78, the facade being rebuilt by Abraham van den Blocke in 1616-17. The building was damaged in 1945, but many items of the interior furnishing have survived. After completion of renovation work a branch of the Museum of the History of the City of Gdańsk will open here. The Court of Artus served as a venue for festive meetings of patrician fraternities. The mannerist portal is decorated with medallions with portraits of the kings Zygmunt III Waza (left) and his son Wladyslaw IV (right). In front of the neighboring house (on the left) at No. 46, there is a porch (about 1760) with decorative slabs created by J. H. Meissner, the most outstanding Gdańsk sculptor of the late baroque era. The reliefs represent Cronos, Minerva and Apollo. The house at No. 43, to the right of the Court of Artus, is the Dom Ławnikow/Councillors' House. Since 1713 it has often been called the Gdańsk Vestibule on account of the art collection of Lesser Giełdziński, which used to be displayed in the great vestibule. Built at the end of the 15th century and rebuilt in 1617, it burned down in 1945. In the course of reconstruction, the facade coverings were removed and a rich Gothic profile emerged. Only the richly sculptured portal and gable of the facade are witnesses to its transformations. In the porch there is the original 18th-century stone slab with the image of an old man. The **Złota Kamienica/Golden House**, also called the Steffens or Speimann House, was built in 1609 by Abraham van den Blocke, and it was not until 1616-18 that master craftsman Hans Voigt from Rostock with his team covered the facade with gilded reliefs. Jan

The Green Gate on the Motława River.

Speimann, Mayor of Gdańsk, book-lover and art collector, had the house built for himself. The figural scenes on the facade show famous heroic deeds, and are accompanied by the busts of eminent citizens, politicians and rulers. Here there are Brutus, Themistocles, but also Wladyslaw Jagiełło and Zygmunt III Waza, and the inscriptions make it easier to avoid errors. By a stroke of luck the facade did not collapse. Held up by special scaffolding, it remained standing until the addition of the remaining walls of the house; the salvaged sculptures were subjected to conservation and the destroyed sculptures were recreated.

The **Brama Zielona/Green Gate** was built by Regnier of Amsterdam in 1564-68 according to the design by Hans Kramer of Dresden, a master builder of those times. The Gate stood on the site of the oldest gate in Gdańsk, the Kogi Gate, dating from the mid-14th century. The palatial character of the building ensued from its intended function – the city appropriated it as the seat of the kings who frequently came to Gdańsk. But only Maria Gonzaga was guest here on the way to her wedding with the Polish King Kazimierz in 1646. The reception given by the council in the grand room in her honor evoked the admiration of the French court that accompanied her. From 1746 it became the seat of the Natural Science Society, established by the famous Gdańsk scholar Daniel

53

On the Long Coast.

Gralath. In 1883 the fourth arcade was opened up at the location of the city scales, and the arms of the kingdom of Prussia were also placed here. Behind the Brama Zielona/Green Gate, the view unfolds onto the Motława River and Wyspa Spichrzow/Granary Island, and in the opposite direction after crossing the bridge you have the attractive view of the Długie Pobrzeże/Long Coast and the Main City. From Granary Island the composition of the urban layout is clearly visible: the closing by gates of the streets leading to the port. The largest gate is the Żuraw/Crane, towering over the surrounding buildings. The segment of the Długie Pobrzeże/Long Coast between the Green Gate and the Chlebnicka Gate is the wharf of the White Fleet. From here ships set out for tours of the Gdańsk port and the Gdańsk Bay, and trips to Westerplatte, to Sopot and to Hel.

The **Chlebnicka Gate** came into being in the first half of the 15th century and is the oldest of the preserved gates. It is characterized by modest forms. At the end of the arcade on the Motława River side we see a stone coat of arms from the period of Teutonic rule – two crosses. The English House at **ulica Chleb-nicka**, also called the Angels' House, was built by Hans Kramer for the English merchant Dirck Lylge. The five-storey building is crowned by a three-storey gable. The dark colour of the lower stone part clearly indicates the state of the ruins before reconstruction was begun. Together with the neighbouring houses it is today used as a hall of residence for students of the College of Art. The Gothic stone facade of the house at No. 14 (from 1520), unique in Gdańsk, also has an unusual history. The heir to the Prussian throne, the future King Wilhelm III, liked it so much on his visit to Gdańsk that he instructed that the deteriorating house be bought. The outstanding Prussian architect K.F. Schinkel oversaw the careful dismantling of the facade in 1822. Then all the pieces were transported to Potsdam onto Peacock Island. There, a specially designed house was built with a facade recreated from the fragments that had been brought over and carefully assembled. In this way, the Gdańsk House was recreated on Peacock Island. In the course of the reconstruction of ulica Chlebnicka it was decided that the facade of the Potsdam original be copied, which was carried out with perfection. This is now part of the student house whose main entrance is in the English House.

The **Church of Our Lady**, the parish church of the Main City, was raised to the status of Gdańsk con-cathedral in 1986. The first priest of St. Mary's parish began his service in 1344, and the present priest is the sixtieth in its history. Of the seven gates, the one beneath the tower is the entrance for tourists. Tradition links the earliest Gdańsk church of this name to the Pomeranian Prince Świętopełk II, who is said to have donated it in 1243. The prince's body lay in state in this church in 1266. The present construction was created in several stages, perhaps on the site of an earlier building. In 1343-60/61 the nine-bay basilica was built (with the nave higher than the aisles, lit by its own windows) as well as a tower reaching the height of the ridge of the church roof. From 1379 to about 1400, the chancel and transept were built, the builder and most probably the designer being Henryk Ungeradin. In 1425-47 his work was covered with roof and gable. Work on raising the tower was begun after the Teutonic Order had been removed from Gdańsk (1454), and it was completed in 1466. In 1484-98 the aisles were broadened and raised to the height of the transept and chancel, creating a uniform hall layout. On February 28, the mason Henryk Hetzel laid the last brick in the dome. Since 1928 systematic conservation work has been carried out. It should be remembered that the interior can hold up to 25,000 people, and Gdańsk had about 20,000 inhabitants at the beginning of the 16th century. The 1945 fire destroyed the medieval rafter framing of the roof, about 40% of the vault fell in. Conservation work has been conducted since 1946. In 1950 the reconstruction of the vault was completed, and 8,000 sq. m. of roof was covered with tiles. The steel construction is about 15% lighter than the wooden one. The consecration of the church took place on November 17, 1955.

The length of the building (together with the tower buttresses) is 105 m and the height of the tower 77.6 m, the vault is 29 m above floor level. The main feature of the church architecture is its scale and at the same time the simplicity and modesty of the decorative details. The huge glass hall impresses with the clarity of the planning concept and the logic of the design. The net vaults with the repeated theme of stars cover the aisle of the eastern part and the nave. The aisles have crystal vaults. The church interior also leaves a strong impression with its wealth of art works collected over the centuries, in moderation supplemented by contemporary works. Thanks to the labor of Gdańsk curators before 1945, most of the church furnishings were dismantled and evacuated outside the city. These objects were rescued from destruction, although not all have come back in spite of much effort. The good state of preservation of the entire interior furnishings is the result of the constant work of conservation teams.

When visiting the church you can see the following works of art (clockwise): the stone Pieta, from about 1410, chiseled by the

The Neptune Fountain on the Long Market.

creator of the Gdańsk Beautiful Madonna (the Chapel of St. Rajnold). »The Last Judgement«, painted by Hans Memling in 1472, on the adjacent wall is only a copy. The original of this fine work, which for nearly five centuries was a jewel of the art collection of the Church of Our Lady, is in the National Museum in Gdańsk. The epitaph of Michal Loys of 1561, an outstanding work of the Dutch school, with alabaster reliefs and fine ornamental paintings on the reverse side of the wings (the Chapel of St. Mary Magdalene) can be seen here. There is also the stone sculpture of the Beautiful Madonna, decorated with polychromy, a work produced in Gdańsk in about 1420, whose creator is referred to as the Master of the Beautiful Madonna (St. Anne's Chapel).

In the northern wing of the transept, on the high wall reinforcement there is the statue of St. George fighting the dragon (15th cent.) and in the background a wall painting of a landscape. Below, on a special screen, there is a painting from the beginning of the 16th cent., transferred onto a new base in the course of conservation work which had uncovered an earlier work underneath it. In the floor of the St. George's Chapel there is the gravestone of Mateusz Zimmermann and Tomasz Tympfius, donated in 1513 and supplemented with a metal shield in 1675. Next to it is the gravestone of the von Werden family dating from the second half of the 17th cent., of Dutch workmanship, the most beautiful of the modern age. High above the heads of the worshippers the sculptor Abraham van den Blocke affixed the figures of the kneeling Bahr couple. In 1620 the mounting of the statue was finished. Opposite the gravestone, in the Holy Cross Chapel, there is the altar of St. Adrian, brought over in 1520 from an outstanding workshop in Antwerp, with the traditional gilded carvings and artistically valuable paintings on the reverse side of the wings. The astronomical clock next to it is the work of Jan Duringer of Toruń, created in 1464-70 and restored in 1987.

The crossing of the nave and the transept is the place with the best view of the spatial layout of the Church of Our Lady, an outstanding work of European architecture. The Main Altar, the work of master craftsman Michael of Augsburg, was created in Gdańsk in 1511-17. Seriously damaged in 1945, it was subjected to restoration, which was completed in 1986. In contrast to the traditional character of the portrayal of the Coronation of Mary, the painted wings of the polyptych presented the newest artistic trends of South-German painting. The group of the Crucifixion in the rood arch was created in about 1517 and is the work of the artist Pawel, the most outstanding woodcarver of the Gdańsk late Gothic

The nave of the Church of Our Lady.

period. The sculpture of Christ is placed at a height of 4.35 m. Next to the left pillar of the rood arch there is the high wooden tower (8.13 m) of the Gothic sacrarium, richly decorated with carvings and polychromy, from 1478-82. The conservation work was completed in 1986. On the opposite pillar the sculptor Abraham van den Blocke placed an epitaph for Mayor Bartlomiej Schachmann in 1607. At the crossing of nave and transept is the biggest decorative chandelier in the church, cast in Gdańsk in the 17th cent. The neighboring chandelier, originally with a statue of Mary, is the work of the artist Andrzej from 1490. Gdańsk artistic craftsmanship was also famous for its foundry work.

The southern wing of the transept has the 1591 epitaph of the alderman Edward Blemke, the work of Willem van den Blocke; it is the biggest stone epitaph in Gdańsk. To the left there is also a stone epitaph of Mayor Konstantin Ferber from 1646, grandiose and with much symbolism. The carved group of the Crucifixion, from about 1420, in the Chapel of the Eleven Thousand Virgins, stands out due to the unique expressiveness of the figure of Christ. The wall paintings in the Chapel of St. Jacob the Greater, from about 1430, were uncovered in 1980 during conservation work. Apart from the monumental figure of the patron saint, an important item is the detailed, though in places barely discernible, passion cycle. The Altar of St. Hedwig in the chapel dedicated to her is of Gdańsk workmanship, from 1435-40. In front of the chapel there are the gravestones of Mayors Konrad Letzkau and Arnold Hecht, who were murdered in 1411 during their mission at the Teutonic castle in Gdańsk.

The southern aisle contains the Chapel of Our Lady of the Priest Confraternity, built in 1335. Dedicated in 1965 to honor the 2,779 Polish priests who were murdered during the Second World War, this is a national commemoration site. The statue of Christ the Sorrowful in red granite, the work of Janina Stefanowicz-Schmidt from 1965, draws on a traditional iconographic theme of Polish folk sculpture. The epitaph of Mayor Jan Brandes and his wife Dorota, from 1586, the work of Willem van den Blocke, can also be seen here.

The main nave has an octagonal baptismal font base with rich, multi-figured reliefs, from 1553-55. The bronze casts of the allegorical figures and the decorative door were made in the workshop of Henry Willemson in Utrecht. The original basin of the baptismal font and the railing were lost in 1945. The baptismal font standing on the plinth is from the Church of St. John in Gdańsk, dating from 1682. From the same church comes the early-baroque pulpit from 1616-17, with interesting paintings by Isaac van den Blocke. The original pulpit, an outstanding rococo work by Johann Heinrich Meissner from 1762, burned down in 1945 together with the great organ ornamented with carvings, also by Meissner. The present frontal view of the organs, completed in 1629, is also from the closed down church of St. John, mentioned several time already. In 1981 a committee for the reconstruction of the organ in the Church of Our Lady was established in the Federal Republic of Germany. The instrument was manufactured by the well-known firm of Hillebrand from Iserhagen, the conservation of the decorative construction surrounding the organ and music

The Church of Our Lady.

The front facade of the Grand Armory.

choir and its reconstruction were carried out by a team of Gdańsk experts. A concert inaugurated this example of good cooperation in 1985.

The houses at **ulica Piwna**, although more modest than those of the Royal Way, are worthy of attention on account of the painstaking execution of the sculpture details and the number of stone porches, into which all the original preserved fragments have been built. The house at No. 1 (the corner of ul. Tkacka), escaped destruction. It was built in 1640 by Andrzej Schlüter the Elder (the father of the famous Gdańsk sculptor). The facade stands out with its rich early baroque stone decoration and the characteristic wrought-iron carpenters' sign, from the second half of the 17th cent.

The **Grand Armory** is a masterpiece of decorative Dutch mannerism. The creator of the design was Antoni van Obberghen of Mechelen, a Fleming who settled in Gdańsk and was a great asset to the city. The main work was done in 1602-5. Abraham van den Blocke was in charge of the sculpture work. The facade is flanked by two small octagonal staircase towers. The niche with the statue of Athena and the date 1605 marks the center of the composition. The upper storey is formed by an attic wall hiding the roof. The wealth of stone decorative details is unique. The large windows considerably lessen the wall area and add lightness to the whole composition of the facade. In 1945 only the walls were preserved. It was decided that after its reconstruction the upper storey would be handed over to the College of Art, and the lower would be turned into a shopping center between ul. Piwna and the Targ Węglowy/Coal Market. On the side of the Targ Węglowy, at the level of the second floor, a passage links the Armory with the Baszta Słomiana/Straw Tower of the 15th cent. Low and wide, with thick walls, the Straw Tower served as a magazine. The Old Pharmacy was later built onto the opposite side of the Grand Armory. This name is a kind of joke, because cannon-balls were made here instead of pills for the sick. The building of the Wybrzeże Theater was completed in 1965 in accordance with the designs of Lech Kadłubowski, in the place of the destroyed theater of 1801.

The English House and the Church of Our Lady.

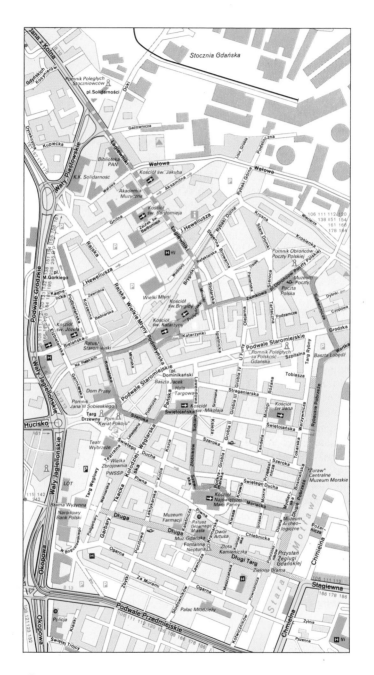

Stocznia Gdańska

Gdyńskich
Kosynierów
Pomnik Poległych
Stoczniowców
pl. Solidarności

Gazownicza

Doki

Podstoczna

Dyrekcyjna

Kupiecka

Biblioteka
PAN

Wałowa

Wały Piastowskie

K.K. Solidarność

Kościół św. Jakuba

Akademia
Muzyczna

Rybaki Górne

Aksamitna

Krosna

Kościół
św. Bartłomieja

Zamek św.
Bartłomieja

Gmina

J. Heweliusza

Rybaki Dolne

Stare Domki

Krośnienka

106 111 112 120
138 151 154
161 166
178 184

Pomnik Obrońców
Poczty Polskiej

Podwale Grodzkie

Rajska

J. Heweliusza

Rajska

pl.
M.Gorkiego

Karmelicka

Zawodna

Korzenna

Podbielańska

Bednarska

Wielki Młyn

Refektarska

Browarna

Sieroca

Obrońców Poczty Polskiej

Muzeum
Poczty

Poczta
Polska

Dylinki

Czopowa

Wały Jagiellońskie

Elżbietańska

Kościół
św. Józefa

Bielańska

Ratusz
Staromiejski

Na Piaskach

Kościół
św. Brygidy

Kościół
św. Katarzyny

Katarzynki

Podmurze

Mniszki

Krosiek

Podwalska

Igielnicka

Zamkowa

Olejarna

U Furty

Tartaczna

Podzamcze

Grodzka

Szpitalna

Baszta Łabędź

Targ Rybny

Warkka

Podwale Staromiejskie

Pomnik Poległych
za Polskość
Gdańska

Podwale Staromiejskie

pl.
Dominikański

Baszta Jacek

Hala
Targowa

Pańska

Grobla IV

Grobla III

Tobiasza

Rożana

Straganiarska

Minogi

Kościół
św. Jana

Rybackie Pobrzeże

Warzywnicza

Dom Prasy

Pomnik
Jana III Sobieskiego
Pom.
"Kwiat Pokoju"

Targ
Drzewny

Kościół
św. Mikołaja

Świętojańska

Świętojańska

Szeroka

Lawendowa

Podmłyńska

Szeroka

Węglarska

Grobla II

Książęca

Szeroka

Kozia

Grobla I

Tandeta

Tokarska

Hucisko

Teatr
Wybrzeże

Świętego Ducha

Złotników

Świętego Ducha

Przędza-
lnicza

Szeroka

Wielka
Zbrojownia

PWSSP

Kołodziejska

Kozia

Świętego Ducha

Bosmańska

"Żuraw"
Centralne
Muzeum Morskie

Wały Jagiellońskie

Targ Węglowy

Tkacka

Piwna

Pończoszników

Kaletnicza

Świętego Ducha

Węglarska

Mariacka

Długie Pobrzeże

LOT

Brama Wyżynna

Narodowy
Bank Polski

Gerbary

Podwale Przedmiejskie

Garbary

Długa

Lektykarska

Pocztowa

Kościół
Najświętszej
Marii Panny

Mariacka

Kleszna

Kiejska

Muzeum
Archeo-
logiczne

Pożar-
nicza

Długa

Muzeum
Farmacji

Piwna

Ratusz
Głównego
Miasta

Dwór
Artusa

Chlebnicka

Stara Motława

Chmielna

Okopowa

W. Bogusławskiego

Ogarna

Podwale Przedmiejskie

Przyrynek

Muz. Gdańska

Złota
Kamieniczka

Fontanna
Neptuna

Długi Targ

Przystań
Żeglugi
Gdańskiej

106 111 119

Stągiewna

Za Murami

Ogarna

Mieszczańska

Zielona Brama

166 178 186

Okopowa

Policja

Kładki

Święte Trójcy

Pałac Młodzieży

Podwale Przedmiejskie

Kołodziejska

Żytnia

Pażenna

Chmielna

106 111 118 120
138 151
178 186

Walk
The Old Town and the Main City

The **statue of King Jan III Sobieski**, the work of Tadeusz Barącz, was set up in 1897 in Lvov, with which the monarch had close ties. After 1945 the Ukrainian authorities gave their consent to hand the work over to Poland, and in 1965 it was set up at the Targ Drzewny/Lumber Market. In the 14th cent. this area was outside the fortification walls, and documents from the 15th cent. show that wood was traded here. When the ramparts were put up in the 16th cent., it was included. The present green space between the triangular square and the fortification walls is the result of the decision taken after 1945 not to reconstruct the houses of this formerly densely built-up area.

Along ulica Kowalska over the Radunia Canal we come to the **Old Town Hall**, built by Antoni van Obberghen in 1587-89. The rather small, compact structure with the slender corner turrets, the dome crowning the roof and the dark-red brick walls that contrast with the delicate and elegantly sculptured stone elements – these are classical features of fine Flemish architecture. The main portal is ornamented with mascarons and the finely sculptured arms of Poland, Gdańsk and Royal Prussia. In the vestibule there is a bronze plate with the bust of Johannes Hevelius (1611-87). Hevelius was not only an astronomer of world renown, but for 46

The route of the walk is marked in grey in the map opposite.

The Old Town Hall on the Radunia Canal.

years he was also an alderman and then a town councillor. Not far from the town hall, on the roofs of three houses at ulica Korzenna, he built a large astronomical observatory. He made the 150-foot long telescope himself as well as cutting the lens. Through dozens of published scientific papers he strengthened the position of Gdańsk science. In the wall of the staircase there is an enigmatic portal of Italian craftsmanship with the date 1517, no doubt originating from the Cracow workshop that functioned at the time in the royal palace at Wawel. During the reconstruction of the Main City Hall at the end of the 16th cent., the portal was

Monument of Jan III Sobieski.

transferred to the Old Town Hall, with the addition of new elements. In the vestibule there is a stone arcade decoration with bas-reliefs of Mercury, Ceres and Neptune, from ab. 1560. This comes from the splendid vestibule of the Conerts' house at ulica Długa 45. Many vestibules of houses of the Gdańsk patriciate were ornamented with similar works, as can be seen in engravings and descriptions. The allegorical baroque paintings on the walls are the work of Adolf Boy from Gdańsk, from the second half of the 17th cent. The nine allegorical paintings on the ceiling were created in the workshop of Herman Han in the same period. The middle picture contains the figure of Zygmunt III Waza.

On our return to the Radunia River, we come past the **Wielki Młyn/Grand Mill**. It was built in 1350 by the Teutonic Knights, and until its destruction in 1945 it generated energy by using the Radunia waterfall. In the roof there used to be six storage floors. Since its reconstruction in 1961 it has served as a storage house and now houses shopping centre.

The **Church of St**. **Catherine** was built in stages on the site of an earlier church, most probably from the 13th century. In 1326 work was begun on the triple-aisle chancel, and in about the middle of the 14th century on the aisle body and the lower part of the tower, which was raised in 1486. The splendidly developed dome of the tower (1643) was to compete with the dome of the Main City Hall. It burned down in 1905 and was rebuilt in 1908. After 1945 the church was rebuilt, with the entire vaulting being reconstructed, and in 1979 the reconstruction of the dome was completed. A group of Gdańsk citizens living in Hamburg and Lübeck financed the set of chiming bells that play every hour. Inside, the Gothic triptych (1515) of the Old-Town butchers' guild has replaced the destroyed main altar. Two paintings from this altar have survived, both by Anton Moeller: The Crucifixion with the general view of Gdańsk in the background (1610) and The Last Supper. The Crucifixion group in the rood arch was done by the Gdańsk sculptor Pawel in 1510. The Renaissance enclosure of the baptismal font, the work of M. Gletger from 1585, is situated in chapel under the dome.

At ul. Katarzynki, opposite the southern facade of the church, stands the Dom Kaznodziejow/Preachers' House with a triple facade, built in 1599-1602 by Anton van Obberghen.

Now we come to the **Church of St**. **Bridget**, built for the Bridgettines in the 15th century, originally double-aisled. In 1514 the south aisle was added and in 1616 the tower was built. The reconstruction following the war devastation was completed in 1975, and the church serves the shipyard workers. In the heated days of August 1980, the Church of St. Bridget was a refuge for the striking workers. In the courtyard of the Gdańsk Shipyard priests listened to confessions, conducted services and preached, giving moral support to the shipyard workers. The church interior is unplastered and rough, with contemporary furnishings. The late-Gothic group of The Crucifixion in the roodarch and the painting The Apotheosis of St. Bridget by H. Han from the mid-17th cent. are an exception. The church is certainly worth visiting, however, because many of the symbols and works of art are in close connection with the dramatic struggle of the workers for human rights and the legalization of the Solidarity movement and its activities, which were illegal.

From the church, it takes you ten minutes to walk along the streets of Mniszki and Łagewniki to plac Solidarnosci Robotniczej with the **Monument to the Killed Shipyard Workers**. It was designed and built by the Gdańsk Shipyard workers after their

The Church of St. Catherine.

victorious strike in the August of 1980. It is devoted to the memory of the workers shot to death on the streets of Gdańsk and at the shipyard gate during the revolutionary strike in the December of 1970.

The route of our walk leads between contemporary buildings of the district towards the plac Obrońców Poczty Polskiej. The name of this part of Gdańsk, Osiek, is known from the 14th cent. The inhabitants of the oldest settlement (in the vicinity of Zamczysko) who survived its conquest by the Teutonic knights in 1308 moved to this area.

71

The building of the **Polish Post Office** was erected in 1838-44. In the beginning a hospital was located here, and from 1925 the Polish Post Office No. 1 and the Post and Telegraph Central Office of Gdańsk. On September 1st 1939 at 4:45 a.m., formations of police, the SS and paramilitary organizations attacked the building, which was defended by the postal workers. In the afternoon the artillery was brought into the fighting and the building was set on fire with flame-throwers. Six postal workers were killed, six wounded died, and the director of the post office died, hoisting up a white flag after 14 hours of resistance. Four defenders managed to flee, and 39 were executed on October 5th, 1939. On September 1st, 1979, a monument was unveiled. In the building there is a small museum on the history of the Polish Post Office in Gdańsk from the 18th cent. to 1939.

Opposite the post office there stands the baroque building of the former alms-house for orphans and the aged (1698-99) and next to it an even more modest building.

Between the houses there is a passage to ul. Sukiennicza, which lies next to ul. Dylinki. These are the grounds of the former **Zamczysko**. Here archaeologists from the Institute of the History of Material Culture of the Polish Academy of Science conducted long-lasting archaeological work from 1945 onwards. They uncovered 17 culture layers from the first settlement, described in a document from 999 as urbs Gyddanyzc (the town of Gdańsk). Archaeologists also located remains of a brick Teutonic castle. The most interesting findings from more than 1,000 years ago are now in the exhibition of the Archaeological Museum next to the Mariacka Gate (on our promenade route). To the right of ul. Sukiennicza the open space (built over before 1945) makes it possible to see fragments of the fortification walls of the Main City, built after its foundation in 1343. The tall (36 m) Jacek Tower visible in the distance marks the place where the fortification walls turned towards the south. In the foreground there stands the squat baszta Łabędź/Swan Bastion, built in place of the baszta Rybacka/ Fisherman's Bastion on the site of the Teutonic castle pulled down in 1454. The small square, rather empty today, bordered on one side by a row of reconstructed historical houses, recalls only by its name **Targ Rybny/Fish Market** that from the Middle Ages this was once the Gdańsk fish trading center. The embankment street Wartka runs along the Gdańsk Shipping office buildings (the landing stage is at the Brama Zielona/Green Gate) to the »Kubicki« restaurant, which sailors once frequented before the war. The customers are different today, but the pre-war style and

Monument to the Killed Shipyard Workers.

quality of the cooking have been retained. Next to it are remains of a medieval bastion and fortification walls. These are the last fragments of the fortifications of the Teutonic castle preserved above ground level. They have survived due to the fact that houses were built here later. After 1945 their ruins were removed and the historical relics uncovered and restored.

73

Granaries on the Ołowianka Island.

From the area of **ulica Wartka**, the old port of Gdańsk is visible. Numerous engravings, from the 17th century on, depict the port with a forest of masts of various types of sailboats and Vistula barges. Here the loading and unloading of goods used to take place, of which much was stored in granaries (there were over 200 of these) situated on Granary Island and Ołowianka. Today this is just a memory of days gone by, but remnants and symbols of the old port still remain: the gate of Żuraw/Crane towering over its surroundings, three granaries on Ołowianka Island and the steam-ship moored on its shore. Together they form the Central Maritime Museum complex. Already in the 19th century the Gdańsk trading port was moved closer to the shipyard area, on the Martwa Wisla/Dead Vistula. On the other side of the Motława, the oldest historical Gdańsk electric power station, established in 1898, still functions today.

The Crane Gate on the Motława River.

The promenade route along the Motława, stretching from ul. Wartka all the way to the Zielony Most/Green Bridge near the Brama Zielona/Green Gate, was formed gradually. In the Middle Ages there were wooden platforms only near the water gates that closed off the streets of the Main City. In about 1400, the platforms were expanded along the bank in order to facilitate mooring for the increasingly numerous ships. It is known that in 1611 there was already a continuous wharf from the Brama Zielona/Green Gate to the Żuraw, and in 1861 this included the entire Pobrzeże Rybackie/ Fisherman's Wharf. Today's appearance of the Pobrzeże Rybackie (from ul. Wartka to the Straganiarska Gate) and the Pobrzeże Długie/Long Wharf (from the Straganiarska to the Zielona Gate) is the result of the last modernization.

The **Straganiarska Gate** was created in the last quarter of the 15th century and was rebuilt in 1958 for housing purposes. It is the youngest of the medieval gates, with a beautiful triple emblem on its facade. In the southern annex on the side of ulica Straganiarska lived the prematurely deceased Zbyszek Cybulski, a movie idol of the 1960s, to whom a memorial plaque is dedicated. **Świętojańska Gate**, from the end of the 14th century and rebuilt in later centuries, was handed over to several clubs in 1977 following reconstruction. From under its arcades we can see the massive St. John's Church (once a parish church, currently not in use). The church was built in about 1350 and was expanded in the next century. It played an important role during the removal of rubble from the Main City. Here all the historical stone elements taken out of the debris were kept, identified and sorted; from here they were transported to conservation and masonry workshops, then on to be used in facades of buildings.

The house adjacent to **Żuraw** on the, northern side, with three gables, was built as a boiler-house for heating the entire district. This kind of architecture evoked the protest of advocates of reconstruction. Today, it houses the offices and workshops of the Central Maritime Museum, and Żuraw constitutes part of the exhibition. As early as 1363 there was a gate here closing off ul. Szeroka. The present shape of the Żuraw was created in 1442-44. Over 40% of the walls and the whole wooden construction were destroyed in 1945. Rebuilt in 1957-59 according to designs by Stanisław Bobiński, the reconstruction work was carried out by the Monument Conservation Workshops. The huge wooden wheels in the central part of the building were also reconstructed. In their interior, workers treading on the rungs moved the mechanism of the crane, which served not only for loading and unloading, but also for raising masts. It is worth visiting the interior of the Żuraw and looking over this mechanism. The museum entrance ticket includes a ride on the ferry to **Ołowianka Island**, where in three restored granaries with the names Oliwski, Miedż and Panna there are museum exhibitions on the history of the port of Gdańsk, on the Vistula shipping, or of objects from historical wrecks found in the Bay of Gdańsk. The Workshop of Underwater Archaeology is an important supplier of exhibits. Finally, it is worth visiting the first Polish ship built in the Gdańsk Shipyard, the SS »Sołdek«. Gourmets may be interested in the reconstructed historical »Pod Łososiem« restaurant (established in 1704), at ulica Szeroka 52. The reconstruction of the medieval **Brama Św. Ducha/Holy Ghost Gate** was completed in 1987 for a publishing agency. However, the houses on the southern side of ulica Św. Ducha were not rebuilt, in line with the reconstruction plans for the Main City. Thus, the houses on the northern side now get the sun, and the

76

The Church of St. John.

inhabitants have access to the nearby recreational area. In this street were born Arthur Schopenhauer (1788), the famous philosopher, and Daniel Chodowiecki (1726), graphic artist and painter.

Ulica Mariacka is a street worth looking at. The entrance from the Długie Pobrzeże/Long Wharf is of course through the Mariacka Gate, dating from about 1485, which after reconstruction served as the Archaeological Museum together with the neighboring Natural Historians' House. A stone plaque with the arms of Royal Prussia, Poland and Gdańsk ornaments its eastern arcade, while situated on the opposite side are the beautiful golden

View across the Motława River onto the town.

arms of Gdańsk. From here you probably get the most beautiful impression of Gdańsk: the narrow street framed by two rows of slender houses with richly decorated gables and high porches, followed in the distance by the mass of the Church of Our Lady. It is from here that we can see the size of this edifice, the decorative gables and spiry corner turrets. The houses near the church barely reach up to half the height of its windows. As in the past, the street is covered with granite cobblestone and in the evening is lit up by the sun, creating a special atmosphere. This spot is beautiful and charming early in the morning on a summer day, in the full sunlight of a hot noon, or on a snowy or rainy day in winter. In the summer, the colorful umbrellas of cafes and bars, which also serve their guests on the front terraces, provide a shield from the sun's rays. On a cold day, a warm and cozy corner can be found in any of them. The light visible through the half-open doors invite visitors to walk in, down the stairs under the porches, where there are many shops with amber and silver products, replicas of old arms, artistic smithery products and other objects. Contemporary art enthusiasts will find galleries. Time is spent in peace and quiet, away from one's cares. This spot is probably the best present to the people of Gdańsk and to the visitors from the architects, masons, sculptors and monument conservators, who in the years 1956-73 carried out full reconstruction. Here the spirit of the old Gdańsk has been preserved, which was fought for by the ulica Mariacka defenders against the advocates of modernism as early as in the 19th century. Today's ulica Mariacka is also a monument expressing gratitude to all the past generations of Gdańsk people.

The House of the Natural Science Society, today the Archaeological Museum, is adjacent to the Mariacka Gate. Built in 1597, most probably by Antoni van Obberghen, it was destroyed in 1945 and only the outside walls have been preserved. From 1845 on the house was the seat of the Natural Science Society and although for several decades it has now served a different function, the traditional name is still sometimes used in recognition of the achievements of these predecessors. The permanent exhibition of the Archaeological Museum – findings from the oldest Gdańsk stronghold – deserves special attention.

The porch of the house at ul. Mariacka 29, opposite the Museum, was built after 1945. On entering the terrace, you can see a mounted fragment of an original baroque slab, which apart from the old photographs and design drafts was the starting point for designing the gypsum model of the porch slab in a 1:1 scale. The models were made by the best sculptors from the State School of

The Mariacka Gate.

Art in Gdańsk. The house at No. 1, by the church, presents Gothic forms from 1451 in a brick facade, the remaining walls are of frame construction. There are two high (2.7 m) stone porch slabs that stand out, depicting the Annunciation scene and dating from the beginning of the 16th century. The models were prepared by Prof. A. Smolana on the basis of the fragments found and the studies of architect M. Kilarski. The neighboring house at No. 2, although rebuilt again, presents modest baroque forms from the middle of the 17th century not only in its facade, but also with its original Dutch bricks taken out from ruins, cleaned and used anew. The porch is from the first half of the 18th century and its slab with the Good Samaritan is partly original. The slabs of the porch at no.

Coat of arms on the Mariacka Gate.

52, the seat of the Polish Writers' Association in Gdańsk, are the original ones from the end of the 17th century, restored. The facade is from 1569. On the gound floor is one of the best galleries of contemporary art.

To the right of the house at ul. Mariacka 52 is the Parish Church of Our Lady and the **Royal Chapel** complex. The lower, unplastered parts of the side walls are relics of the medieval Meat Benches. In the narrow passage between this complex and the church (the official name is ul. Plebania), the last authentic facade of a Gdańsk Gothic house of the 15th century has been preserved nearly entirely. The neighboring facade contains a modest baroque portal of the 17th century with a stone slab in the lintel with the arms of the founder, parson Maurycy Ferber, later Bishop of Warmia. In 1517 he instructed that a cartouche be embedded in the wall with the family crest, three boar's heads, on it. This was the first year of the Reformation in Gdańsk. The nearly two-century old conflicts over priestly functions performed by Catholic priests in the Church of Our Lady led to the construction of the Royal Chapel. With the development of the Reformation, which also had its dramatic episodes in Gdańsk, the reformed community and the pastors obtained greater possibilities of influence. In accordance with the traditional settlements, the guardian of Our Lady's parish was the king, which had an impeding effect on the elimination of Catholic priests and practices from the church. However, this did

The Ulica Mariacka.

not solve the problem in Gdańsk, where the Reformation triumphed. Archbishop Andrzej Olszowski, Primate of Poland (died in Gdańsk in 1677), during his visit to Gdańsk offered a considerable legacy for the construction of a new church, and Jan III Sobieski added the remaining amount. Five houses were bought at ul. Św. Ducha, and in their place, the only baroque church in the Main City was built. The royal architect from Warsaw, Tylman of Gameren, drew up the plans, which were realized by the Gdańsk builder Bartlomiej Ranisch in the years 1678-81. Stepping back from the facade into ulica Grobla IV (broadened after 1945) makes it easier to analyze the original facade of the Royal Chapel. The architect made an effort for the construction not to disturb the rhythm of the structures in these narrow streets (today the houses no longer exist that used to fill out the now vacant spaces on the southern side of ulica Św. Ducha). He therefore designed a small pilastered facade, flanked on both sides by facades of houses, which created a screen for the vestibule and chancel. Only the dome on an octagonal drum towers over the surrounding houses. The sculptures of the facade are the work of Andrzej Schlüter the Younger. It contains interesting mascarons and a large heraldic cartouche.

We walk along ulica Św. Ducha towards the Targ Drzewny/ Lumber Market. In the house at No. 45 (in today's numbering), called the Turtle House (about 1650), there once lived Joanna Schopenhauer, author of a moving diary that has been published and mother of the philosopher Arthur Schopenhauer, who was born here on February 22, 1788.

We now retrace a few steps and turn into ulica Kozia. In the distance we can see the massive building of the Church of St. Nicholas. It is believed that the beginnings of the church go back to the twelfth century, and that the founder was Prince Sambor, founder of the Cistercian abbey in Oliwa. It is a fact that in the year 1227 the Pomeranian Prince Świętopełk brought over from Cracow a Dominican convent and gave to it the **Church of St. Nicholas** at the market square. In the year 1235 the church and monastery were visited by King Władysław Łokietek. At the level of the foundations of the present vestry, fragments of that first church have been discovered. The construction of the present church together with the monastery was begun after 1348. In the year 1487 the interior was decorated with a star-shaped vault, then the towers were raised higher. The annual Dominican Fair, which takes place together with the church fair on the day of the patron (August 4th), was established in 1260 by a bull of Pope Alexander IV. In the year 1835 the monastery was closed down and the property confiscated. In 1840 the monastery was dismantled, but after 105 years, in 1945, the Dominicans returned. Fate had been kind – the church had not been burned down and all the rich furnishings, typical for the interiors of Catholic places of worship, were undamaged. The early-baroque main altar, from 1643, with a painting of the Coronation of St. Nicholas is most probably by a northern Italian school. In the chancel there are fragments of a Gothic painting (from the first quarter of the sixteenth century) with a passion theme and seating for the monks from those times,

The Ulica św. Ducha.

which had been expanded in the middle of the eighteenth century. The altars by the pillars between the aisles as well as the remaining furnishings of the church interior are the work of Gdańsk artists of the eighteenth century. In the southern aisle there is a beautiful, richly ornamented enclosure of the baptismal font, dating from the year 1732. Under the choir there is a nobleman's tombstone, a rarity in Gdańsk, of Jan Konopacki, who died in Gdańsk in the year 1591, while accompaning the entourage of Zygmunt III Waza.

On the neighboring square, **plac Dominikański**, there stands a trade hall from the year 1896. The hall and market square were built in place of the old monastery houses and the garden that reached up to the fortification walls, still partly preserved to the east of the square. The 36 metres high corner tower of the Main City's fortification walls (from around 1400) also served as an observation tower. Its name «Jacek» is connected to the first Dominican abbot in Gdańsk, Jacek Odrowąż, who in the course of time was canonized.

Excursions

The excursions cover those sights which do not present themselves on the two walks described in the previous chapters.

Excursion No. 1

The **Holy Trinity Church** at the street of the same name is located in the Stare Przedmieście/Old Suburb. The Franciscan Order came to Gdańsk in 1419. Shortly afterwards a chancel and two wings of the monastery were built. The St. Anne's Chapel was built in 1484. The chancel was raised higher in 1495, and the triple-aisled hall was completed in 1514, the western facade ornamented with the most beautiful late-Gothic gables of the city. In 1555 the departing monks handed over the monastery to the town council of Gdańsk, which located a school here, the Gymnasium of the Town Council, later called the Academic Gymnasium. The Franciscans returned to the church after 1945 and rebuilt the destroyed chancel, and since 1991 restoration work has been carried out on the house from the first half of the 17th century which separates the church courtyard from the street. Inside is the late-Gothic church pulpit from 1541, with a canopy from 1617. On the eastern wall are the wings of two late-Gothic altars, painted in the first quarter of the 16th century in the studio of master painter Michael, creator of the painted scenes on the main altar in the Church of Our Lady. The five great heraldic cartouches from the vault keystones are from 1514. On the walls and pillars there are richly ornamented brass reflectors, which are characteristic of Gdańsk interiors of the time. These were executed in the second half of the 17th century, as were the chandeliers in the nave. The Chapel of St. Anne, adjoining on the west side, was where the Polish reformed community gathered, while Polish sermons were preached by lecturers from the Academic Gymnasium.

Left: The monument on Westerplatte.

Excursion No. 2

The **National Museum** is at ul. Torunska 1. It is located in the old Franciscan monastery, later used by the Academic Gymnasium. The collections were started by Rudolf Freitag (1805-90), sculptor and Professor of the Gdańsk School of Art, who contributed much to Gdańsk culture. Following general repair work and the refurnishing of the house in Gothic style in 1867-72, the Municipal Museum was opened here. In 1885 the collection of the Museum of Arts and Crafts was added. Seriously damaged in 1945, it was opened after reconstruction in 1948 as the Pomeranian Museum. Since 1972 it has had the status of a National Museum. There are permanent exhibitions on the folllowing topics: Pomeranian Gothic art, medieval fabrics, Dutch and Gdańsk furniture, Dutch and Gdańsk painting, Polish painting, Gdańsk silverware and artistic smithery.

Excursion No. 3

The **former Polish Gymnasium** at ul. Jana Augustynskiego (the name of the school principal of the time), is housed in the former barracks building of 1910. Founded by the Gdańsk Macierz Szkolna (an educational society) in 1922, it was in use as a school until August 29, 1939. Over 500 students attended it during this period.

Excursion No. 4

The **Stone Sluice** is at ul. Grodza Kamienna in the Old Suburb. It was built in 1619-24 during the regulation of the Motława River, in accordance with the designs by Willem J. Bening and Adrian Olbrants of Holland. This water engineering device still functions, ensuring the flow of water into the Nowa Motława Canal. The closing of the sluice causes the Żuławy depression area to flood, which makes access to the city difficult. This measure was used with good results many times. The neighboring bastions of Żubr/Aurochs and Wilk/Wolf are a fragment of the city's former fortification ring, built in 1621-36 according to designs by Kornelius van den Bosch of Holland.

West gable of the Church of St.Trinity.

Excursion No. 5

The former **home of Günter Grass** at ul. Lelewela 13 is in the district of Wrzeszcz, east of the Gdańsk-Wrzeszcz railway station. The modest house from the turn of this century was quickly restored after 1945. On October 15, 1927, Günter Grass was born here, as the son of colonial merchant Wilhelm Grass and Elzbieta née Krause, from the Kashubian village of Bysewo. This outstanding German writer is tied to Gdańsk not only by birth, but also by a feeling of belonging there, which he has expressed in »The Tin Drum« and other works. Here in Gdańsk he is very much esteemed and has many friends.

Excursion No. 6

The **Gdańsk Główny railway station** is built in neo-Renaissance style, dating from 1900. The tower is 48 m high. In spite of modernization, especially of the underground infrastructure, the mass of the building, the main halls and the functional structure have not been changed.

Excursion No. 7

The **»Wisłoujście« fortress** lies at the old bed of the Vistula. Its first mention is from 1369. The brick tower of 1482 served as a guardhouse and lighthouse. In 1558-62 the round fortress was built with a two storeyed artillery position and four blockhouses. In 1608 the extensive earthwork was completed. Around the earlier works the fort carré with its large corner towers, designed by Antoni Obberghen, was built. In the 17th century barracks were built inside the fort. The stronghold was subordinated to the town council. It has never been conquered. Today inaccessible, it is visible from ships coming towards Westerplatte or from the area around the moat surrounding the fortress on the land side.

View onto the picturesque Oliva.

Excursion No. 8

The **Westerplatte** Peninsula was formed by the Vistula at its entrance into the Baltic, receiving its final shape in 1846. It can be reached by the ships of the White Fleet from the wharf at the Brama Zielona/Green Gate, by city bus or by car. Due to a resolution by the League of Nations, it was handed over to Poland on a hereditary lease in 1924, to be used as the Polish Military Transit Depot (trans-shipment of ammunition and arms). In 1933 to 34 four guardhouses were built with reinforced concrete cellars, and in 1936 barracks. The garrison numbered 182 soldiers and officers under the command of Major Henryk Sucharski. On September 1st, 1939, at 4:45 a.m., the first shots of World War II

were discharged from the battleship Schleswig-Holstein. Bombarded also from the air, the defenders surrendered on September 7th, when ammunition and medical supplies ran out; 15 people lost their lives. Military instructions had only provided for a 12-hour defense. The monument unveiled in 1956 was designed by Franciszek Duszenko, the general layout was by Adam Haupt. The granite monument, which is 25 m high, stands on a 22.5 m high hill. From beneath it there is a panoramic view of the harbour, the district of New Port, Gdańsk, the North Port (1970-76) and the sea coast all the way up to Gdynia.

Oliwa Cathedral.

Excursion No. 9

The **house with the arcades in Lipce** is situated at ul. Jedności Robotniczej 297 (the road to Tczew and Bydgoszcz). The oldest of the typical Żuławy houses, it dates from the first half of the seventeenth century. The half-timbering used to be filled with clay, nowadays bricks are used. The wall on the other side of the road borders onto the canal, which was built from near Pruszcz to Gdańsk in 1338.

The interior of Oliwa Cathedral.

Excursion No. 10

Oliwa is an important item on the sightseeing list. In 1186 Prince Sambor gave Oliwa and six villages to the Cistercians from West Pomeranian Kolbacz. The monks not only built a church and monastery buildings, but also developed agriculture on their land. At the Potok Oliwski/Oliwa Stream, which came from the Wyżyna Gdańska/Gdańsk Highland, they dammed the water in many places, building mills, oil mills and sawmills. From the 16th century on the Gdańsk patriciate built their mills, fulleries and smithies here. In the 17th and 18th centuries, numerous manor houses and palaces were built by the patricians along today's ulica Polanki. In 1860 Oliwa had 2,000 inhabitants, and in 1874 it obtained city rights. The first mayor was Jerzy Czachowski. In 1926 Oliwa was incorporated into Gdańsk.

The **Holy Trinity Cathedral** in Oliwa was originally a wooden chapel built in 1188, when Prince Sambor settled the Cistercian monks there. In about 1200 the oratory was built, which took up the first two bays of the current chancel, although it was much lower. The attacks of the Prussians in 1226 and 1236 and the murder of the monks halted the construction work. In the middle of the 18th century the transept was built and the three-aisle nave, which was soon extended. From 1350 on the church was enlarged to the present dimensions. The vault was built after 1577. In 1831 the monastery was disbanded and the church was taken over by the parish. In 1925 the Gdańsk diocese was established, and a year later the parish church was raised to the status of cathedral. The domes burned down in 1945 and were rebuilt in 1971.

The Church of Oliwa is a triple-aisled basilica with a transept and an aisle around the six-bay chancel. The length of the structure is 107 m, the height of the nave is 17.7 m. The entrance leads through the baroque portal of Abbot M. Hacki, from 1688. The present furnishings of the interior were created after the fire in 1577. The great organ was built in 1763-88, the instrument was made by Jan Wulf of Orneta, the organ design was carved by the monks Gross and Alanaus. In the summer season organ concerts are given here. The northern aisle has a gravestone of the aristocratic Kos family, from 1600, chiseled by Willem van den Blocke; the marble baroque altars are from the second and third quarters of the 17th century; the painting »The Coronation of St. Mary« in the altar of the second bay was painted by Herman Han after 1624. The northern arm of the transept has a wooden altar from 1606, in mannerist style; the baroque stone altar was donated by Abbot J. Grabiński in 1635; the stalls with bas reliefs of the four Evangelists are from the end of the 16th century. The chancel aisle contains an altar donated by the abbot M. Hacki in the third quarter of the 17th century and a painting by H. Han »The Birth of Christ«; in the southern arm of the transept is a symbolic tomb of the Pomeranian princes from 1615; opposite is the tombstone of J. Hulsen, chiseled by J. H. Meissner in 1760. The chancel has a rococo pulpit, from after the 18th century; opposite are the epitaphs of the Oliwa abbots K. Geschkau (d. 1587) with the painting of »The Last Judgement« and D. Konarski (d. 1616) with

The Abbot's Palace in Oliwa.

his portrait. On both walls, in a decorative casing, there is a gallery of the abbey's benefactors, with paintings by H. Han. The monumental stalls for the monks are from 1604, the work of the monastery workshop. The main altar was donated by Abbot M. Hacki in 1688. You can also visit the monastery cloisters. Located here is the Room of the Peace of Oliwa, commemorated with a marble plaque, where a peace treaty was signed between Poland and Sweden in 1660, following the long war of succession.

The **Abbot Palace** today houses a modern art gallery of the National Museum in Gdańsk. Built by Abbot Jacek Rybiński in 1754-56, the palace was rebuilt after the fire in 1945 with full reconstruction of the interior. The palace wing was the seat of the abbot in the 15th century. On the other side of the lane is the Abbot Granary from 1723, with an ethnographic exhibition. The former abbot park is now the A. Mickiewicz Park. The southern part in

French style was designed by K. Dębinski in 1760. The romantic northern part was designed by T. Saltzman in 1782.

The **Oliwa Zoo** was established in 1954 in the Tri-City Landscape Park, among gentle slopes covered with forests and vast meadows. The natural habitats of animals occupy 30 hectares (about 75 acres), and the recreational grounds 70 hectares (about 170 acres). The recreational facilities are good, and the zoo can be reached by ul. Karwieńska.

Excursion No. 11

The name **Tri-City** came into being after 1945 to designate the city agglomeration of Gdańsk, Sopot and Gdynia; each of the cities has its own separate administration. The number of inhabitants is close to 800,000. The municipal railway operates on the route from Tczew to Wejherowo, making it easier to commute to places of work. The transit route for cars is via the ring road from Pruszcz Gdański to the northern part of Gdynia. Each of the cities has its own individual features. Gdańsk, apart from the voivodship authorities, has six colleges of higher education including the polytechnic and the university, as well as the philharmonic and the opera. Sopot, known as a resort, became a city in 1901. It has the best recreational facilities, the longest boardwalk in Poland, between the beaches and the Opera Leśna/Forest Opera. The latter is popular not only for its annual song festival, but also for its attractive location among hills and wooded walking routes. Gdynia is the youngest city, as it only received city rights in 1926. The necessity of organizing sea transport for the nation, which did not regain Gdańsk in 1918, led to the construction of the port and city. The Gdynia shipyards compete with the Gdańsk shipyards, there is a fishing base here, two colleges of higher education and a music theater famous in the whole country. The houses of the main streets are characteristic for European architecture of the 1930s.